ALL TH_
GARBAGE OF
THE WORLD,
UNITE!

전 세 계 의 쓰 레 기 여
단 결 하 라

KIM HYESOON
Translations by DON MEE CHOI

ACTION BOOKS NOTRE DAME, INDIANA 2011

For Margot,

Stay healthy and happy!

Thank you so much for your friendship.

Love
Don Mee
10/5/2012

ACTION BOOKS

Joyelle McSweeney and Johannes Göransson, Editors
Eli Queen, Art Direction
Kimberly Koga, 2009-2011 Editorial Assistant

The Action Books editorial offices are at
356 O'Shaughnessy Hall, Notre Dame, IN, 46556
and are distributed by Small Press Distribution (spdbooks.org).

Visit us online at actionbooks.org, actionyes.org,
and montevidayo.com.

Action Books is grateful to the Daesan Foundation of Korea
and to the College of Arts and Letters, University of Notre
Dame, for their instrumental support of the translation and
publication of this edition.

TABLE OF CONTENTS

The ether of a poem, the emptiness, the poesy exists inside the move-
ment of language. The trace of the movement can only be drawn as a
formless form, like the way our brain activities reveal themselves as waves,
the way electric currents flow between you and me. I'll call such wave
motion the "moving dot."

The moving dot can be extinguished in an instant, yet it contains all
information, even eternity. Try placing a dot on the undulating waves. The
moment I extend my arm, the dot is already gone.

The moving dot is infinitely small because it moves, yet at the same time
it is infinitely large. Inside the infinite smallness the self becomes infinitely
tiny and dies. Inside the infinite largeness the self becomes infinitely
huge and dies. The extremes of the infinitely small and infinitely large are
the non-self. The non-self is required by the speaker and the listener of
a poem. Poetry is a modality that follows the path of the discourse and
through that path is able to conceive an empty space. To say that the dot
does not have form or even a size because it is infinitely small is no differ-
ent from saying that the dot is infinitely large and therefore is the universe.
The moving dot is the slowest, yet the fastest. It is as big as Chuang Tzu's
bird and as small as Chuang Tzu's fish. The moving dot is a whale's body
and the egg of an anchovy.

The moving dot is the "now, here, and I" that appear in poetry. All the images in poetry become instantly compressed inside the "now, here, and I"—the moving dot. The chaotic, the marginalized, the "now, here, and I" flutter about in the fringes—the "now, here, and I" pulls the moving dot with its breath. The tiny moving dot breathes in the swirls of the Milky Way and pulls the fringes of the city of Seoul. The images of poetry are the trace of the moving dot; they point to the place in which the eternity that can be extinguished in an instant is caught by the text. The images extend the days they'll exist inside the moment of absence. Conversely, they extend the days of the absence inside the moment of existence. The trace of the moving dot is an infinite world—a world beyond time, a world rediscovered, a world of poetry. It is a sketch of something sublime beyond existence, beyond the grave. In spite of that, poetry exists inside a single woven text. Poetry exists inside the text that I experience, inside the expanded, multiple space that I, the object, must overcome. Poetry exists inside prose's maze of suffering, the neglect, the fringe, the repetition. A woman goes, passes along the windy road of language, a woman without a mother-tongue, a woman who labors in no-action—she goes.

The inside of the maze is a path of to and fro, a spiral path and a dead end, a path that is far yet near, a sky path, a water path. Like the inside of a conch shell, like being swept by a whirlwind, a typhoon. What stories does the maze tell? Does it speak to future generations about life's journey, the roaming, the difficulty of finding an exit, or perhaps the recollection of a struggle at the crossroad? The maze is the diagram of the trace that is both present and absent. In the lines of the maze, life and the world intersect. The lines form a crack that crosses the two worlds. The maze is either a map of the nomads who roamed the desert looking for a path, or a drawing of the trace of my footsteps on magnificent Seoul.

The maze is a passage through which life's secret is delivered. The passage looks like the moments of my rites of passage. Therefore, my maze is a record of my endless escape, my running away. In order to escape from the maze, I must realize that time does not flow in a linear fashion; time is spread out. The inside of the maze is filled with dead ends and paths that lead me back to the exit. I don't know how far I must walk, but there is a dance, the rule of an undulating movement.

The footsteps of someone who dances inside the maze seem confusing at first, but the steps connote the essential rules of the infinite undulation. They contain immanent rhythm that leads to plentitude and a new structure. The maze's breathing overcomes the masculine, the overly regulated rhythm that denies any repudiation, the prose narrative that follows linear time, the gravity—the modality of dancing steps that unravel. Its only criterion is indefiniteness and fortuity. As the maze grows more complex, it contains the flexible logic of non-alignment. This logic of non-alignment demands from me a new experience with language. I must go beyond my conventional prose in order to attain the experience of the new. But when I enter the newness, once again, I become constricted by the rhythm and repetition of verse. I bend language on both sides to build a diction that undulates in a new way. Only then can poesy enter, transcendent, inside my poem.

When such shape is pulled into the inner world of divinity, it becomes a mandala. The mandala is a drawing of an archetypal self. It brings the inside to the outside. Emptiness is made visible by the mandala. Time is compressed in the mandala—from birth to death, the rise and the fall of sun and moon, and eternity.

However, the law of fabricated linear time is imposed on history, including my life. Some of the literary writings that emerge from the law of fabrication include manifestos, autobiographies, historical fiction, and poetry without poesy. These writings do not vomit what the humans have eaten but strange dolls instead—dolls with their faces. They sell their souls to

ix

the linear fictionalization. Inside linear time, a butterfly that passes in front of my eyes can never be seen again. However, like the mandala, poetry does not exist inside such linear time. Several subjects exist equally, simultaneously. These things dream of conversing with each other, and the conversing becomes a subject in itself.

I am many inside poetry. "I" as a subject, the cognizant "I" is deconstructed. I have never once lived as a single "I" inside poetry. The confusion of the multiple "I" is what makes me write poetry. I am a mother, a young unmarried woman, an angel, a prostitute. I am an infant just born, an old woman near death. When I am a mother, "I" the young unmarried woman is ill, and when I am a young woman, the mother is ill. Like the children who defy school and run out of the gate, multiple "I's" dangle from the open skirt of the Buddhist Goddess of Mercy. "You" inside poetry also dangle from the skirt.

My writing floats around the inside and the outside of me. Like a dog who has lost its owner, I follow the scent of this and that person, asking whether they are me. At such moments the poetic discourse is plural. The suffering multiple "I's" are merry. Their merriment rescues me from the forgetfulness of existence. Without merriment, poetry remains on a singular plane. In order to achieve polyphonic planes, my poetry needs to be merry—inside things, between things, inside the multiple "I's" and between the multiple "I's".

I sing, my skull sings, the world sings, the stars sing. The songs are all different but connected by merriment. The music is already within poetry.

As a woman, I observe the identity inside me that rises and falls, waxes and wanes, lives and dies like the moon. Therefore my body's form is infinitely fractal. I live according to the way that fractal form is read, feeling the path through which life flows in and out. I love, therefore I become myself. I see the "I" inside you.

x

As a woman I open my body not to men but to the context of eros. Such love has spilled out from my body before the beginning of time and it is from there that my voice of existence bursts forth. The essence of my existence does not have a fixed form; it has a moving form, always circulating but never repeating itself.

Therefore as woman, as poet, I dance and rescue the things that have fallen into the coil of magnificent silence; I wake the present, and let the dead things be dead.

Kim Hyesoon 김혜순
Previously presented at
American Literary Translators Association (ALTA) Conference
October 21, 2006

TRANSLATOR'S NOTE

"American domination—the only domination from
which one never recovers. I mean from which one never
recovers unscarred."
– Aimé Césaire, *Discourse on Colonialism*,
trans. Joan Pinkham (New York: Monthly Review Press, 1972).

A while back, I submitted a short poem by Kim Hyesoon called "A Hole"
to a U.S. literary journal. The editors were interested in publishing it, but
they asked if I could change the word "hole," which recurs throughout the
poem, to something else because it had negative connotations in this cul-
ture. I was too busy trying to finish up some other work then, so I politely
said I didn't have the time to think about it. Now that I've had some time
to think about this whole matter, I can finally say something about it. To
change "hole" to something else would mean changing the world "A Hole"
came from. During the Korean War (1950-53), about 250,000 pounds
of napalm per day were dropped by the United States forces. Countless
mountains, hills, rice fields, and houses were turned into holes. Four mil-
lion perished, leaving more holes. It's a place that is positively holely. Kim
Hyesoon's hole poem comes from there, and so do I. At school, I was
taught that Korea looked like a side view of a rabbit. Its severed waist
stitched up with barbed wire, its scorched belly studded with a million
landmines, its adorable ears branded as an axis-of-evil. As a defect, I
don't know how to affect something else other than bunny cartography.
I'm not being polite. I'm pleased to be able to offer you more hole poems
by Kim Hyesoon.

Don Mee Choi
Seattle, 2011

xiii

ALL THE GARBAGE OF THE WORLD, UNITE!

YOUR FIRST 당신의 첫 2008
& Manhole Humanity 맨홀 인류 2009

HORIZON
지평선

Who split [×a word]
the horizon?
The mark of the division between sky and land
A night when blood water seeps out from the space between

[Space = word.]

Who split
the space between the upper and lower eyelid?
The mark on my body from the division between outer and inner vastness
At night tears spurt out from the space between

Can only wounds permeate one another?
The dusk descends as I open my eyes → darkness
A wound and another wound merge
so crimson water flows endlessly
and the exit called "you" shuts in darkness

[Avoid the light — a pair eyes paradoxically to the darkness.]

Who split
the white day and the black night?
She becomes a hawk by day
and he becomes a wolf by night
We pass each other like knife blades
the night we meet

1

SAND WOMAN
모래 여자

The woman was pulled out from the sand
She was perfectly clean—not a single strand of her hair had decomposed

They say the woman didn't eat or sleep after he left
The woman kept her eyes closed
didn't breathe
yet wasn't dead

People came and took the woman away
They say people took off her clothes, dipped her in salt water, spread her thighs
cut her hair and opened her heart

He died in war and
even the country parted somewhere farfar away
The woman swallowed her life
didn't let out her breath to the world
Her eyes stayed closed even when a knife blade busily went in and out of her

2

People sewed up the woman and laid her in a glass coffin
The one she waited for didn't arrive, instead fingers swarmed in from all
directions

The woman hiding in the sand was pulled out
and every day I stared vacantly at her hands spread out on paper
I wanted to get on a camel and flee from this place

In every dream the woman followed me
and opened her eyes
the desert inside her eyelids was deeper and wider than the night sky

STARFISH
불가살

I leave my starfish in the Pacific Ocean
my cuckoo in Tibet
my sloth in the forests of the Amazon
and I cook and lecture and age like this

I tie my fingers to a pine tree in the tundra
and bury my eyes beneath the snow of the North Pole
and leave my heart to melt in the abyss of the Pacific Ocean
and I cook, eat, sleep, drink, and even laugh like this

Therefore sadness blows in from Sumeru
Cold tears arrive from the bottom of an ice sheet that stays frozen
all year long
Therefore fever arrives from the Sahara
from a faraway place overgrown with cacti that can't close
their mouths, for needles stick out from their tongues
the inside of my open mouth is hot as lava

So don't keep coming to me, my starfish, crazy starfish
It is said that you were made from a fleck of rice
and can become as big as a house, a mountain top

4

Don't return here even if a ditch forms from the tears
that I shed every night missing you
the ditch is no place for you to live
If you keep coming back I'll pin a star to my hair
and all the nights of the world will explode inside me

A fine new day arrives like a clear sky after the typhoon
When I stand in the street, wearing a pair of dead gutter-rat shoes,
my butterflies blow in from all over even though my body is so small
Why are my arms, my head, my legs so distant?

I must have been chased by all the wind in the world and gotten wrecked
inside this body
My arms and legs dissolve in all directions
my head feels hazy

Since I always lack oxygen, my footsteps move across the tundra
Being on time is my sickness, but I need to get going to be on time

Someone stares into me for a while then flees
My feet are outside of my vision

My feet gradually fade away and
take off like wolves into the distant mountains

Starfish [*Pulgasal*] is the name of a monster from a fable, a
monster that can only be killed by fire. According to the fable,
during the Chosŏn period (1392–1910 C.E.) when Buddhism
was suppressed by King Yi Sŏng-gye, monks were imprisoned.
One monk created an animal from a fleck of rice, and the
animal escaped from the prison and roamed the entire country
eating iron bits and turned into a monster. In Korean *pulgasal*
and starfish are homonyms.

SEOUL, KORA
서울, 코라

The mountain barks
then follows me

The mountain gives birth
The mountain licks a mountain
The mountain's litter sucks on its nipples
The mountain cold-heartedly discards all of its litter
The young mountains copulate in broad daylight, the stench
The mountain roams like the pack of dogs inside a maze

The mountain looks at me with its wet eyes
It trembles as I stroke its neck
The mountain gets dragged away with a rope around its neck
The mountain gets locked up behind bars. It's beaten. It's kicked.
It dies.

6

The mountain eats shit, eats a corpse
The mountain, the rash-covered mountain attacks me with its flaming eyes
The mountain, the snow-topped mountain cries
The mountain without a single tree laments with its head flung back
towards the sky
The mountain bites and fights a mountain
The mountain, the big mountain chases its own tail

Empire's military exterminates the mountain that swarms
The mountain that survived, the mountain, the mountain climbs over a
mountain
and runs away
It's still running away

The mountain, the mountain that wants to shed a mountain, brings
its hands together and stretches them towards the faraway mountain,
touches its forehead, pulls them down to its chest, looks at the faraway
mountain once again as it draws its elbows to its waist, then bends its
right knee, both hands down on the ground, then bends the left knee,
presses down its hands on the ground and then stretches them out,
then prostrates, its entire body touching the ground. Then it cries. The
mountain circles a mountain, repeats the whole thing every three steps.

Kora refers to a loop of prostrations around the sacred
mountain, Mt. Kailash, in Tibet.

7

RED SCISSORS WOMAN
붉은 가위 여자

Confusion on who the "her" is

That woman who walks out of the gynecology clinic
Next to her is an old woman holding a newborn

That woman's legs are like scissors
She walks swiftswift cutting the snow path

But the swollen scissor blades are like fat dark clouds
What did she cut screaming with her raised blades
Blood scented dusk flooding out from between her legs

The sky keeps tearing the morning after the snowstorm
A blinding flash of light
follows the waddlewaddling woman
Heaven's lid glimmers and opens then closes

How scared God must have been
when the woman who ate all the fruit of the tree he'd planted
was cutting out each red body from
between her legs

8

The sky, the wound that opens every morning
when a red head is cut out
between the fat red legs of the cloud

birth – sky
femi-ized,
maternal

(Does that blood live inside me?)
(Do I live inside that blood?)

That woman who walks ahead
That woman who walks and rips
with her scorching body her cold shadow

New-born infants swim
inside that woman's mirror inside her as white as a snow room
the stickysticky slow breaking waves of blood
like the morning sea filled with fish

TO BAKE A STAR
별을 굽다

Got off Line 4 at the Sadang subway station to change to Line 2
Got on the escalator, turned around and came upon a crowd of faces
They were all like red clay masks
How many kilns must have baked all those faces?

Somewhere inside those expressionless faces
was it the hidden power that makes our eyes open each morning?
Hiding the power that makes the ground deep inside ebb
too deep to be heard from the outside?

There must be someone who crouches at the corner of every constellation
firing up the stars in the kiln
and fate's starlight blessed by that someone must reach the earth
but the ground that caves in
like falling water is too deep
so the starlight can't reach here

Inside those many people
the heat invisible from the outside must be wavering
There must be a kiln inside everyone that
holds up the body that wants to return to mud

The faces have been baked like that for ten, twenty, fifty years
so all these faces must be red clay masks fired from the inside

ONION
양파

Under the faucet a man peeled a woman's skin
The woman cacklecackled and peeled easily like an onion
As a layer of dark night peeled off transparent day soared
Blood draindrained down a pipe
like the mushy inside of a fresh egg
Someone cried, stopitstopit why are you all acting this way?
When day gets suckled the sadtastingspicytasting night soars
Day and night kept this up for a thousand ten thousand years, for all
eternity
yet the woman peeled layerafterlayer
The man who peeled an onion cried because of its sap
and the woman cried along with him
ah andsoregardless today's day left and night arrived
yet I didn't know where I was
maybe I was hidden somewhere between the spicy layers
so when I kept asking where I was and turned around
the woman's body was just as before
and the man kept crying and crying and peeled the woman's skin
After I was all peeled like an onion, I wasn't there anymore
but the I that used to call me I was hiding somewhere
Night hid and trembled under the wood floor after taking off its spicy skin

12

yet the sea endlessly took off and put on a pair of pants
and yet it was hotinsummer and coldinwinter and everything drifted away
Isn'tthisthemostbeautifulstoryintheworld?

THE LANDSCAPE'S GAZE
풍경의 눈빛

I thought I was gazing at the landscape
but I was startled the moment I realized that the landscape
was staring at me instead

As I went up the steps of the castle
I thought the landscape would look different as my field of vision changed
but it was as though I got slapped in the face the moment I realized the
landscape had shifted its gaze and had been watching me all along

The girl who tugged at my wrist and said she'd show me around the
castle suddenly screamed as she went up the steps
When she awoke from her nap, she felt as if millions of men had
surrounded her and were looking down at her
We suddenly understood each other and screamed at the top of our
lungs.

The girl stopped crying like a tiny bell that could fit inside a brass mold
Then she was trapped by the arrows of the landscape flying in from six
different directions and began to suck on her dirty fingernails
She hid inside a cocoon like a larva
forgetting that she had begged for money to show me around

Beneath the balcony of the castle
the hell that belongs to those unborn had spread out
It's a lie, it's a lie, everything's a lie, said the wind
and flew into the vast bogus landscape
Birds fell off as if to slap my face and descended to lower ground
With each step the landscape's shifting gaze
fell and whirled in like glue sniffed from above below in all directions
enwrapping my whole body

FIRST
첫

The thing that I envy most in the world is your first.
The thing that you envy most in the world—I wouldn't know.
Your first that seeps out from your sleeping face.
The thing that you brought here when you came from there.
I want to cut off your first.
What thing inside your face do I envy?
What thing? I wouldn't know.
Perhaps a thing like the very first milk from your mother who made you.
Your first that is made from such an ingredient.

You open a photo album and look at your first. The first inside the photo is
probably thinking of you. Thinking that it is thinking of you. Your beloved
first is hiding inside the photo but your hand floats the train on top of the
open field of the computer keyboard and touches first, first, first, first,
each train car. Your first. Where is it hiding? Your first that is shy and hot
as steam from mommy's milk that spouted into you long ago. Your first
that shuddered lumplump and became your body. The tickle you felt
when you met your first like when a flock of geese flies into the sunset.
Because you are now writing a farewell letter to me, your first is laughing
quietly? Perhaps it is thinking harder about you inside the photo? Your
first terrifying solitude that used to crouch and hang onto the inside of

mommy's tummy. First love that used to share and eat such solitude. There is a knife inside the hearts of all the firsts of the world. There is nothing that is more heartless than first. First always dismembers. First forever dies. Dies in an instant as it is called first. A wedge of your lip that first has severed then runs away. First, first, first, first. Your two wrists without a body run alone above the train tracks of the keyboard, you and your first. A dog with two necks barks and roams, searching under the hazy moon. The forgotten didn't know it was forgotten. Died. Your first is dead. First that still flaps about inside your forehead.

Your first, my first, firsts that part forever.
I approached you as if
I were meeting you tonight for the first time
and had lost my first.
Did you also?
Then shall we hold hands and kisskiss?
Should I say it like that?

And at that time your first is the finale, flower, fracture.
Died. D e i d. Dide.
Shall I say it like that?

BALSAM FLOWER
봉숭아

A child who licks the doorsill's dirt on her finger
turns around
A child with red eyes
I who have not yet left
Where did the palm of the hand go that slapped the child?

So deeply buried
that the pink fingernails
still wiggle beneath the rocks
The teeth of the old days
that used to bite the nipple

Why doesn't Mommy's womb open? Why is it sealed shut?

Tonight the sky, the coal tar ceiling
flutters like a Tibetan black tent
The salty star gets saltier as it cries
The salty stench from the body
is boiled and becomes stronger every night
A red awl pokes me urging me to get out quick

18

LADY PHANTOM
LADY PHANTOM

There is a corpse in the room
I killed someone
I left the corpse and came here to have a drink
It's so amusing
to keep the people who are laughing and chatting
from finding out that I've left a corpse in the room
I tell them a story I've made up
saying it's the latest joke in town
Maybe no one here has left a corpse behind
Everyone's boisterous as if they have no bodies to hide
Somewhere in the tavern
a one-eyed bog opens up
like a white goat's shiny eyeball
I place a chair on the eyeball and sit down
Did I really kill?
The room seems distant like in a dream
A beak stained by blood
pecks at the heart of someone who's been burnt
and by the time the feet submerged in the dark bog
are cleaned with a dirty feather
the corpse's legs are already cold

Why did I set fire to the room and scream
then throw water on that someone's body?
The eyeball stays open like a puppy that waits
for its owner all day in front of the door
Did I close the eyeball?
I'm anxious
I can't stand myself
I who am getting boisterous
I need to grow my fire hair again
I need to go out and kill myself again

BENEATH MOUNT SUMERU
수미산 아래

A rock swells out of a rock
on the faraway mountain
the rock barks woof woof then retreats
Soon after the rock closes up

A dog, its whole body, swells out of Buddha's face
at the temple beneath the mountain
and barks woof woof then retreats
The instant a tranquil smile lands on Buddha's face
I can see a mouse being chewed up inside Buddha's lips

In the blue sky that peeled off layer after layer
the dog that had been smoked all day
barked woof woof sadly as though it were spewing out fire
then it ran off after turning the snowy mountain red
and at the temple beneath, the water in an iron pot
bigger than a lake boils gentgently
The sky's whitestwhite pack of dogs
falls into the iron pot

21

The wild dogs that come out of me cry all night long outside the tent
I beg plead and bark
Please let me in I want to go inside
When I open the tent to look up at the moon, the dogs' saliva
drips down white upon all the valleys of the mountain peaks

I can hear the voice of someone I dislike in my throat
At the temple beneath the mountain, Buddha's torso shrinks
every time I bark wo oof woof
Now the golden Buddha has become as small as a toad

ECHONATION
매아리나라

Here light comes from faraway then goes back
Here wind comes from faraway then goes back

Here lightlightlightliight dries up
Here windindindindiind sweeps away the leaves

My feet are caught in the trap set out by the land
like rats stuck inside a sticky rattrap

Here in echonation a distant place arrives from somewhere then leaves

In order to forget my body
in which you remain
I carry my bag
and walk far far far across the desert

Teacher leaves for somewhere faraway
suddenly the scene ends, a black out

Only the saliva dripdrips into the mouth
like a statue with a busted stomach

23

As I fell screaming, deep inside the water
from deep inside, I heard the voice of someone who couldn't shout

Dear Head, do you want to leave this heavy body?
Dear Heart, do you want to discard this heavy body?

My feet, my feet, my feet, my feet
get myfeet myfeet myfeet my feet out of here

Clickclickclick cicadas land on my face and cry out
Most likely no one can remain here

SILK ROAD
비단길

I paid a visit to my fever during my break

Here I carried a baby on my back and kisskissed it
As the flesh scent that smelled like gourd flower slowly ripened
a message intermittently arrived saying that my suffering was boiling in
that place all alone, covered by the stench of urine and feces
under the scorching sun
I who have concealed that place am going inside it
like a camel that pantspants showing all of its gums
Suddenly the fever came for me and pounded my insides and left
leaving a few words on a thin piece of silk that could melt
but later...... later...... as I ripened to mush
Out of the blue, after many decades, I went to visit my fever

In the desert the crazy sun
like the terribleterrible hydrogen bomb that is still going off
after it exploded in the year of my birth
pours out the shards that still glow from red to dark
I have never once received the touch of the rainwater
The old camel was carrying me up the black hill
where the rocks that had broken into pointed bits of quartz were piled up

I who have broken out in red spots
between the layers of fine silk
The white twigs that the camel had no choice but to chew
had thorns as thick as my fingers
and blood gushed out nonstop from the camel's mouth
I couldn't believe there could be such a place filled only with suffering
My daughter said that inside the mirage she saw
a Buddha that had attained nirvana
stretched out on its side inside a temple
but I had to swallow the tall deep-blue waves
that kept coming up through my throat
Every time I swallowed the waves, the red sand twister whirled inside me

There was a child who couldn't eat and sleep crying on the bed in the
emergency room
The child was so bandaged there wasn't any opening for the needle, the
tranquilizer and the mother called out the child's name nonstop, 24 hours
a day
Yuni, Yuni, trying to pull the child's name from its body

After I got back from the desert I was lying on the bed in the emergency
room overcome with fever and I stared at my camel that was still climbing
the rocky black hill
I'm here, yet I watch the dirty camel climb the Flaming Mountains by itself
I tell the camel as I shudder, You go there and I'll go here, then at some
point we'll meet again at a pond near the sky
Inside my sleep, feverish, I gulpgulp down the blue mirage on my own

26

I DON'T ROT BECAUSE I'M CRAZY
미쳐서 썩지 않아

The tepid bath water in the tub speaks
You are completely soaked in me
I feel every part of your body
like the music that goes inside your ears
but where are you?

The cooled water in the tub speaks
I've lost my hair
I'm bald
I don't have any smell either
but now I rot like this
through your smell

Music speaks
I don't have arms or hands
I can embrace even your sweat pores
but I can't catch you

I rot because of you
like the bath water
I curl around you and come out and die
like the soaked music

I die because you have forgotten me

The putrid water that comes up to your neck rots

Yes, finally it's the victory of the gutter!
It's the sky of guts! Hurhurray!
The tunnel beneath my feet!

ALL THE GARBAGE OF THE WORLD, UNITE!
전세계의 쓰레기여 단결하라

Someone is missing

On the seat you left, two beer bottles, a cigarette butt, two pieces of
scratch paper.
Why are you screening my calls, my messages? Don't you have anything
else to do?
You are the bourgeoisie of communication. Why am I always so afraid of
the phone?
When you look at me, I always feel as if I should change into something
else.
How about changing myself into a pile of clothes dumped on the sofa
or a pale pink wad of bubble gum dangling from someone's lips
like the poor tummies of all the animals that flail about when they are
turned over?
Do you know?
Eyesnavelgod. Forearmsearflapgod.
Sweetpotatokneesappleseedgod. Pigstoenailschickgod.
Dreamingdivingbeetlesashtreegod. Lovelygirlsheelstoenailgod.
Antsghostscatseyeballgod. Ratholescatsrottingwatergod.
Mrsdustingarmselephantgod. Salivadropexplodeslikefreongas.
Salivafountainevenmoremortifyingnauseatingthanthesmellof-
lionsrottenbreathgod.
Do you know all the dearest gods that are hanging onto our limbs?

29

On the seat you left, a wet towel, a wad of gum, a crushed tomato.
Dear blackgarbagebags who thankfully lent each one of their bodies.
Dear foldedarms of the window and concrete and steel under my feet.
How high the armsofthemachinehammers that beat down steadily upon those foldedarms.
All the pigs of the world unite god. All the cats of the world let's become a butter god.
Dear wrists escape from the arms god. Heap of curses, mackerel corpses spit out from a soccer player's mouth god. There are 3 million gods in India. How many people live there?
Dearest multiple gods that have swarmed in from the sky, land, sea.
On the seat you left, I sit like a garbage god, and do you or don't you know
that I wait for the green truck heading to the landfill like the dearest dirtiest loftiest god that has survived till now because of its hunger for humans?
Do you or don't you know that every day our hair falls and mixes with the melting water of an iceberg in the faraway sea?
Yournostrilssingledropofapricklynosehairearthgod!

STRAWBERRIES
딸기

A full plate of red tongues arrived

They quivered like the tongues of the choir members as they sang the hymns

Your tongue is placed on top of my tongue

Our tongues are getting goose bumps

We examined all sorts of tastes in the world, we returned at last
and gently bumped against the millet-like protrusions

You were like someone who had in your mouth only a tongue and no teeth

The achy root has spread between the intestines like lightning
and the coldestcold stream water flowed down your hair like electricity

I was afraid that the red water would rise if I bit down on the red things in my mouth that my face had vomited endlessly, so I just kept them in my mouth

The four arms as soft as the branches with snow on them became entangled and gathered up a full plate of kisses!

I heard that all those tiny protrusions were my seeds only after I had mashed your tongue

A CHRISTMAS MORNING'S TRUMPET
성탄절 아침의 트럼펫

The naked angels took a foam bath inside the clouds

God lay down next to them wearing a feminine napkin

The eagles that fed on human flesh dripped down like a dirty tattoo
sticking onto the backs of men

They wanted to become angels, but they were so strong
that they became scary animals instead

Children wearing roosters' crowns followed those animals around

Moulin Rouge dancers hung bells from their crotches
and lifted up their legs

Married women who aborted their babies got this reply:
Avoid getting scratches on their eyeballs so not to lower their resale value,
don't break their fingers, don't let them get stained while you put on their
makeup, and do cherish them. I would like to tell you not to worry about
the change in the skin color. The skin will turn slightly yellow, but it's not
a serious problem. Just be sure that you don't remove the doll's makeup

with a nail polish remover and such because white or green stains can appear shortly

As soon as Jesus was resurrected, he got employed as a janitor who sweeps up the countless fake Jesuses manufactured at solemn factories and sends them to an incinerator

The snowman born yesterday was wiped out overnight

Even the bones of the snowman got stolen from the grave

I sent a Christmas card that said, "Virgins who are like a swirl of happiness bursting out every time I breathe. However, it's taboo to show them to old women." I got a reply back, "You swallow the virgins and spew out carbon dioxide every time you breathe, yet you speak pretty well."

All the mirrors of the world held the hands of the sunlight that circle the earth and glimmered for a bit, and I posed in front of one of them as if I were in labor giving birth to a baby hidden inside the mirror

It was advertised this morning that it's most delicious when the angels are melted and used as a spread for bread

An angel who finished her bath screamed a 5 minute-long scream then returned

KNIFE AND KNIFE
칼과 칼

Knife loves a knife

it loves in the air like something without feet

The knife that has fallen in love is not a knife but a magnet

The knives' persistent gazes tug at each other and spin!

The drops of sweat disperse, the moans are spit out

It looks as if the two knives are going to lie down for a bit with their bodies crossed in the air, but their glittering eyes stare out in the same direction, somewhere remote

The moment they beat down on each other's body and aim for a hidden place,
inside their gaze the beheaded cherry blossoms fall off every April!

The knife's love will only end when someone's body ends up on the floor

It can love without any rest like the dancer in red shoes, but it can't end its love

It can endure embracing the blue body, but in the end it can't part from it and go back

It can't come down or even fall down in the air

Blood spews out from the four stiffstiff knees

That body like mine is a hole, cut out that black hole, stab it till the inside overflows to the outside

Wash your face with the warm blood spewing out from the hole

This dreadful love never retreats no matter how much you scream

That is why my love keeps the blade's body up in the air

How shall I say it, that our love's feet never once touched the ground?
Is this a blessing, the fact that our love still hovers in the air?

HUM HUM
웅 웅

The confessional's window looks like a beehive
The holes in the priest's mic also look like a beehive, they are all hexagonal
Every time the priest says blahblahblahblah
a swarm of bees falls out of his mouth
The smell of incense grows overpowering as the alter boy lights the
incense on cue
and the middle-aged choir ladies sing Ave Maria in unison with the priest
The ladies' mouths are all hexagonal-shaped
The saliva inside their mouths is sticky like honey

My mommy's voice is heard intermittently
between the swarms of bees pouring out of the receiver
Drivecarefully anddontdrinkandpartyaround andblahblahthisblahblahthat
When I turn around in the middle of the call and shout
Mute the TV
I see swarms of bees pouring out in the news my husband is watching
The fluttering wings of the bees on asphalt
where rain is beating down
I wonder how many bees live inside the motorcycle
that is carrying a bowl of noodles
I can't stand those bees

Bees swarm from the news announcer's throat
The bees' stingers cloud up the TV screen
As the swarms of bees fall out from the police officer's walkietalkie
the swarms that have lost consciousness pour out onto the closed eyes
of the motorcycle guy who is lying on the ground in the rain
In the rainy night the bees transmit the words in the air in a frenzy
Did the butterfly net burst, did the monitor burst, did my skull burst also?
I can't stand it everythingislikeswarmsofbees likeswarmsofbees

Swarms of bees swarm inside the words that begin with D
Dearpriest Dearteacher Dearjudge Dearmadam Dearuterus Drum D D D
washing machine

The washing machine is spinning hum hum
The fetus is suckled clean inside mommy's tummy
When I put my ears against her tummy, I hear the cries hum hum
the infant's kicking spinning
The priest instructs
Please recite Ave Maria five times before you leave
The confessional's window looks like a beehive
The two earflaps of the priest who peers out from the hole are like
hexagonal gelatin
The priest's black eyes squirm like two bees that have fallen into honey
their two sets of six thin legs wiggling about
Please leave quickly!
hum
hum

GHOSTMARRIAGE
혼령혼례

There is a country where kites that have flown away live together

In that country the whitestwhite threads pour down at night

It must have been the naked body colder and tougher than silk

The night when the whitestwhite naked body unravels itself and turns the
spinning wheel endlessly

The lace writings of the distant past come down from the sky and
anesthetize us stiffstiff

The night when the nuptial song inside the body had to be taken out by
emphatic sign language

There is a country where lonely faces that used to look out into the
distance face each other

As the cautious laughter fallfalls like tiny wildflowers in the dark hollow
space between two faces

the bus carrying the well-wishers slides on the snowy road and rolls over and at night they grow distant from each other, layered with the whitestwhite wedding veils that erase the body when they're worn

There was the whitestwhite invitation card sent from the country where the kites that have flown away live together

The night when whitestwhite writing comes down from the black paper to erase my black writing written on the whitestwhite paper

THE COLD
감기

We gazed at each other from a different world
It was as though I were in the black and white photo that you were
looking at

It is always cold inside your photo
The cough-trees stood coughing along with the river

Whenever I opened my eyes I was on the path to the snowy mountain

I barely made it around the corner and there was still more of the
whitestwhite snowfield
the steep cliff had an endless sheer drop

The night when I look into your eyes, wide open as the frozen sky

A rumor spreads that a ghost is bringing a contagious fever into the village

The smoke from every chimney trembled frantically

You are not inside me, I chased you out

There was an avalanche inside my heart, so I trembled for over an hour

As the cough-trees quivered and shook off clumps of snow
the shards of ice bounced out of the exposed valley

I sat on a frozen bench with the wind against my bare face, my lips
shivering

I wanted to get out of the photo that you are looking at

HEART
마음

Water that flutters along with the leaves of the sheer pink flowers
Water that is feeble from being anxious about the pistil and stamen
Water of the body inside is like the fish-smelling mirror that reflects me
Water that reflects then vanishes in a blink of an eye
Water that mixes with the wind then scatters and wets the hair
Water that submerges me like a cloud that has reached the floor
Water that writes on my body like calligraphy in pale black ink
Water that shakes me gentgently with its waves
Water that spreads on the whitestwhite piece of cotton drying in the sun
making a shape of someone's face I miss then stops
Water that gets swallowed with a pill
Water that strokes the window in the evening then leaves
Water that becomes the fish's breathing inside a fish tank

Water that boils divinely in the middle of the room
Water that wets the fragrant tea leaves
Water that is drunk solemnly, in utmost propriety, facing one another
Water that gathers in the bladder after it cleanses the intestines
Dirty water
Rotten water that boils
Water that forms droplets in every pore of your skin

43

Salty water

Water hits the water. Water is entangled like a snake. Naked water. Water beats the water to death. Water's fingers slapslap. Water crawls. Water rolls about. Water hardens like metal. Water pours down unable to hold back any longer. Water gets written on the cheeks then flows down behind the ears. Water sits in front of water, they reflect each other, then leave. In the water, the shadows of everyday pile up neatneatly. When the damp mirror dies I will also die—that kind of water.

(Water boiled all day in my mouth)

TRAINSPOTTING
트레인스포팅

As I stood at Tongni Station
I felt as if I had become that retired actress
who ran out onto the railroad tracks because her red dancing shoes
wouldn't come off
at a whistle stop where no one gets on or off

When it was time for the express train to pass
the whistle stop had goose bumps like the fishing boat that received a
storm warning
and the mountains that sweated profusely spat out heaps of coal

The fact that even the whistle stop talks
The fact that the whistle stop wakes up from sleep, sweating from fever
The fact that the whistle stop even goes for a walk along the tracks deep
in the night
The fact that the whistle stop also falls down under the dark tree and
weeps
The fact that the whistle stop sits in the corner of a tavern and pretends to
be waiting for someone
The fact that sometimes the whistle stop doesn't answer the phone

Will you let me off at Wedding Station?
or give my regards to Birthday Station every year
and if you don't want to do that, perhaps you could come to
my Funeral Station
Even here the cell phones ring nonstop

The sound of the hundreds of insects passing by all at once
sleepthengo crythengo drinkcoffeethengo haveadrinkthengo
furthermore throw away several train cars and go like an unmarried mother
discarding her baby
then when the whistle stop calls out Let me go with you! no one will turn
around

The tickets from Seoul to Kangnûng have rusted yellow
inside the ticket box with many drawers
and I stare at the tracks quivering like a cello
that has grown infinitely tall
and when the freight train pulls on my loose string and lets go of it
the cold stars appear on my face and it starts to tingle
With my eyes I swallow every wooden block of the track that lies
like a corpse, that used to ride the endless shadows
as though I am unscrewing every screw of the metal band of my watch

WHEN PETALS BLOOM AND FADE
꽃잎이 피고 질 때면

What if the petals bud? What if they itch? What do I do now that all the plants pucker their green lips because it's spring? Between your knock knees, between your puckered lips the leaves are budding through the holes, all the holes in the world, what do I do? I'll crawl to the green field to mash it up. This bright green sea. I'll plug all the deep holes. Inside the green there is rotting water the corpses spew out, the bitterest blue, tannic darkness, red fishiness, lips minty yellow, so I'll chew and swallow all these deep faraway-sky-grassy-green holes. I'll crush them all and smear my body with them. In front of the people who tied my hands and feet and threw my meal into a dog's dish, I'll mash the fields, mountains, wide green sea with my mouth, my hole. The dark eyes are about to open all over my body. What if the flowers bloom? What if the flowering holes of my body itch? I don't have hands to rock-a-bye the blossom to sleep. Every hole in the world has opened and is giving birth. The grassy green field is twisting its hot body, what do I do?

I'mtoldtopray praywithoutanyrest pleadwithmytears obeyalwaysobey since I was born from a hole of this world I'm told to give birth to a hole again but what did I do wrong? If I don't ask for forgiveness I won't be able to go beyond this life I'mtoldtokneel bowmyheadlikeaninsect rubmyhandstogetherandaskforforgiveness getdownlowerandlower kneelandreceiveastreamofurine hitmychestandrepent

47

My mouth foams like a dog pregnant with a litter of twelve pups as down on all fours
I drag my belly along the ground, crushing the newly sprouted grass, knowing or not knowing where I'm heading, whether it's spring or winter, staggerstagger, oh it itches itches

One woman who has become as big as the sky as the land can't fit inside a glance passes by waddlewaddle

THE WATER INSIDE YOUR EYES
당신 눈동자 속의 물

When I get up in the morning singing a sad song
the water in the cup feels sad, the toilet water feels sad
the vase water that gurgles up through the flower stem feels sad
and the water that patiently waits
filling the faucet's mouth also feels sad

Don't say Fly up when you see the birds flying outside the window
because that is really me falling
and falling, endlessly falling
riding the earth that only knows how to fall
into the vast, empty sky

The flowing water washes its body as it flows
but a song as sad as this stagnates inside me
and can't flow out so the stopper cries
and the pipes below also cry

I am a body that is born to flow away
flow away to be born as water inside your body
It's alright that there is no horizon, no land for me to stand on
as long as I just get to go
I don't rest deep inside your body or overflow or whisper
I am born only to remain vacant like the water inside your eyes

Where did this sad song flow in from?
Why does it keep welling up and flowing over my rotting body?
Why does it make the water in my cup, the water in my flower vase cry?
The water rises up so high along the banks of the Han River
that not a single road sign is visible
Down below, deep beneath the riverbed
the sound of cold water flowing inside the underground cave

The ceiling shakes, the columns become wet
and the pots rust. I must open my eyes wide, pump out my chest
and hold my breath and go out
Maybe I need to take some naphthalene, so I won't rot
I need to find the key and get out of here

A BREEZY PRISON BREEZES
산들 감옥이 산들 부네

1-hour-and-30-minute-long prison of my morning commute
Just because there is a window and headlights in front of me
no one knows about this solitary room that runs 70 miles per hour

I go to Room 301 then 401, over here then over there
The 50-minute prison, 100-minute prison, 150-minute prison blow in hard

The cube is even more unbelievable because it's softsoft
The fierce rooms swoop over me
They taste bitter and rancid like unripened chestnuts

Will the prison open
if I peel off those wet eyes stuck to the car window?
Those eyes are lighter than leaves
Those eyes are so resilient
Since those eyes don't peel off
if I pluck a star, a boundless world behind it would open up
that star is a gap but it won't move out of the way because it's crying
so this night, this dark wind tricks me, I don't know that I'm in prison
this night, the prison with a dark curtain flowing down separates you and
me

51

So in this prison you must use emblems
For the prison to forget the prison it must keep telling lies
I rattle off lies in my lecture room

Saying The flowers blossom is to say It smells outside the prison
Saying Let's hold hands is to say I can't escape no matter what
Saying Let's kiss is to ask Did you hide the key?
Saying Sleep with me is to say I'm stuck with a life sentence

Just because there is a window, a wind is blowing, and starlight is leaking
I don't know that I'm in prison
After work when I lie down in my sleeping prison
all the prisons outside of the outside of the prisons run to me
and tie up my body with the redred blood-paths

10-hour-long 10 year-long 100 year-long prison

THE HIDDEN DROWNED BODY
은밀한 익사체

It feels as if I'm inside a uterus when I ride in his car
The taste of having a hamburger and beer inside the uterus!
The taste of waking and slurping up the sound of the radio after I fall
asleep
saliva dripping down my mouth!
The taste of turning over on my side as I lie down after covering myself
with a lace-blanket-like jagged landscape

A whale's cry edited by a small radio station is playing on the radio
and all the cars on the road are receiving different radio signals
How did the whale withstand the immensity of seawater?
It's as though the whitestwhite whale was struck by the submarine's sonar
wave and is being swept up the coast

Long time ago before my time of long ago began
Mommy's stomach was very noisy because it was a major traffic
intersection
After the sprinkler trucks slid into the intestines
a commuter train passed by on top of the blood vessels
and a cruise ship on a rapidly flowflowflow flowing urine river blew its horn

We leave after speaking with our hearts that can only be understood
when we don't speak
in a low-frequency voice that can only be heard if we make no sound
like the way two elephants communicate with each other when far apart
on the remote prairie beyond my light sleep
We speak with our mouths closed as if talking to someone
who drives a different planet like the radio communication
between truck drivers in the snowy night

It feels as if I'm inside a uterus when I ride in his car
The taste of when someone asks, Are you asleep? No! I reply as I toss
and turn and grope for the umbilical cord
then I devour his hands on the steering wheel and call his hands
Mommy! Mommy! inside myself
then get pushed out by the waves of amniotic fluid
that reach all the way to the feet and go back
The taste of becoming far faraway all alone!

The taste of circling his body floatfloating in his thick blood with my eyes
closed in dark pregnancy!
The taste of communicating like the two elephants as we become distant
from one another in different worlds
The taste of driving out into the world for at least an hour with my big eyes
wide open floatfloat floating inside stepmom's stomach!

WHY ARE ALL MERMAIDS FEMALE?
인어는 왜 다 여자일까

I prostrate myself on the floor and kiss my shadow
I bite off the shadow's ear

My shadow's eyes light up

A camel-like person who has never bathed once
hides in my upper body
a black shark-like person who
pulls me into the deep sea and roams about
hides in my lower body

I am a woman who is half eaten by the ancient people
with stinging whips in their hands

Therefore, on my tired face
a camel's eye stays open, bulging out
gazing blankly at the body of my next life
and the voluptuous curve of the sand hill
and hundreds of prickly fish scales
like unborn babies' fingernails
are stuck on my ankles

They never fall off
Someone shakes my arm and wants me to go far away to the desert

Someone ties my legs and wants me to go far away to the ocean

My warm tongue freezes first before my fingers
I stutter, It's cold, it's cold
Menstrual cramps fiercely engulf my lower body
It hurts, it hurts
I twist my body
half of it trapped in the desert
and the rest in the ocean

I bite my shadow's ears
I swim in myself all day

Why are all mermaids female?
Do they self-reproduce?

WHY IS MOMMY SALTY?
엄마는 왜 짤까?

When I wake up from thirst in the middle of the night at Mommy's house
a salt lace curtain droops down the porch window
Patterns made from whitestwhite salt
trail faintly down the wall
When I open the cupboard, the mounds of salt
shine white next to the upside down bowls
and salt accumulates like the first snow of the year on a dress I have
taken off
When I open the attic door for no particular reason
salt pours out one sack, two sacks
When I put a single grain of salt into my mouth
my eyes say, It's salty it's salty, first, instead of my tongue
and two cold streams of water dripdrip
All my life I've done the best that I could, biting my lips
But, oh, what's all this again?
Outside the window a whitestwhite mountain of salt shoots up highhigh
as if there is no end to the sky and suddenly the glass in my hand
shatters into bits
and as Mommy starts to wake up
the salt patterns that spread in all directions
vanish without a trace

like the multi-colored sand mandala that is drawn and erased by the
Tibetan monks
all the salt gets swept into the deepestdeep night sea
Why is Mommy's house so salty?

DELICATESSEN

DELICATESSEN

1.

Father raised children
to eat them, of course
Father said,
My children's plump cheeks
are the tastiest thing in the world

My little sister kept a ball of needles beneath her pillow
so she wouldn't fall asleep at night
As a result she became a porcupine
Spines spilled out from her body as soon as she opened her mouth
My little brother became a bat
He only came out late at night and fluttered about
Be quiet when Father is having his dinner!
Tropical fish in the fish tank floated up like puckered lips
Mommy made soup with the red fish every morning
I became a skunk
When I'm disturbed I have a musky cough all day long

Father walked
carrying us in a black bag
Tears streamed out of it
So many tears flowed that it caused a flood
People from the village made a boat from a rubber bucket
and paddled with a spoon
Don't let Father cross!
Father couldn't reach the house because the river of tears was too deep

2.

When we grew up we raised Father
to use him as a broom, of course
We carried Father and swept the ground in the yard
Sometimes we swept snow as well
Father smoked crouched on a dirt floor
His hair became thinner every day

Put the broom back inside!
How repulsive! When I got closer, I saw myself
My hair had thinned, and I was smoking
as I looked over my shoulder

And I raised Father
inside a warm adobe stove
to eat him, of course

TO SWALLOW A TORNADO
회오리를 삼키다

Have you ever swallowed a tornado?
A tornado is supposed to be swallowed through your backbone
My body flips over
my hair becomes as stiff as frozen laundry
and I feel goose bumps down my backbone

When my body becomes tight as a bow I can see everything
Your wound has exploded red so every valley has become a valley of
blood
The blood-red light is the sin of staying alive by feeding on the living
so the red lips are in full bloom above the dark earth

My beloved, the last skeleton beneath your hair is already dead
The rake-like smile of the wind spreads
on the backs of the pedestrians walking hurriedly
God has clawed and gathered up the empty blankets
of those who have departed this world
and lit a blue fire far up above
The world is like transparent silk underwear
you can see right through it

Am I wind's home
or a tornado's host?
When the wind's path that is as cold as a snake
rises up from the deep place
my arms and legs flutter like the bamboo leaves on the day a typhoon
arrives
and when my tears splattersplatter everywhere
a sad song comes up like a whirlwind from the inside of my body
Someone please come and hold my bow-like body
that keeps getting bent back

Have you ever swallowed a tornado?
Have you ever sat by the night sea and cried, I don't want to! I don't want
to!
Have you ever swarmed out to the sea and thrown the pebbles hard
while listening to the waves shout, Take it, take it, take it?
Do you hear all the different screams of the million water droplets?
The spirits that don't want to leave cry so easily
Have you ever closed your fists tightly and withstood their cries?

Have you ever shouted, Go! Go! Go back!

SKYPUPPY
하늘강아지

Warm and soft.
It's like a marshmallow.
The pulse is faint and fast.
It moves quickly across my inattentive eyes.
I might be able to put my finger inside its small pink mouth.
It's the softest thing in this world.
It's so soft that you can't even embrace it.
I must put a bowl of milk out in the kitchen every morning.
Look at it. Its body curls up like a sleeping ball of fog.
Be careful. One hit of breath can make it disappear.
I want to hold it so badly that at sunrise I get a feathery-cloud-like body
ache.
When I stare blankly it's like a tiny transparent ball in front of the kitchen
door.
It might have come out of my body without my knowing.
Could it have come all the way down from the sky to my kitchen?
That thing was so light that it used to fly about in the nine celestial bodies
of the dead before I was born.
Did it return to take me back?
The lightest skypuppy
in the world.

It moves quickly
across my eyes again.

AN OLD WOMAN
나이 든 여자

meme is a lone tree that got planted in a bed
a tree so huge that she can't see her entire body all at once
She's a tree that can't even turn over or rub with her fingers
when the first butterfly she has waited for tickles with its thin toes
the spaces between the grooves of her lips

meme's waist is so wide that she can't bend
over or lie down by herself
Someone must come and change
her underwear and diapers
"But it's alright, please just insert the pencil between my lips"
meme is a big tree
meme—she can get jealous and miss someone, but she can't even make
a single call
When I scratch meme's side it feels as though I am scratching
the thick skin of an old tree!

meme is a lone tree that can't go and die on her own
but loves most the fantasy of closing her eyes tight and curling herself into
a ball and escaping by going under the bed, under the drain, out of the
Earth, swirling out of the sewer

65

mememe is a lone tree
No one can walk beside her with head held up in the air
because of the stench she gives out when she cries before the first leaves
of the season sprout and the dogs lift their legs and piss on her lower
trunk and take off

memememe is a lone big tree
Her stench of sadness when she cries before the first flowers of the
season bloom
is so unbearable that my family members carry a bowl of medicine
and hold their noses outside the door

DOUBLE P–HOW CREEPY
쌍비읍 징그러워

pp they're so creepy that I can't stand it. pappaoppa they are so creepy that I can't stand it. Squeeze hard and have some honey, a gift from pappa, when I opened the lid of the beehive the wigglewiggling larvae filled each hexagonal cell, ahahahah it was like seeing pappaoppa larvae inside each hole of pp. Two of my married former students showed up with their husbands and one called her husband oppa and the other called her husband pappa—how creepy. I had no choice but to say, I'm leaving first I can't bear to hear any more of this kinship name nonsense. I'm so afraid of pp that I don't want to say happy or cute. I just feel great! great! I don't clap, yet I bite the emptiness. Maybe I'm a princess who has to live with smiles dangling from my face to keep my kingdom peaceful. I even hate soappy laundry because I hate pp. In my dream the washer is spinning roundandround, the wooden laundry stick beats down on the laundry splashsplash, and Mommy's scream gets sucked into the washer as she pulls her adorable babies out of it and throws them onto the floor. Whenever I dream this dream, I feel as if I'm pregnant with a wet-laundry-like baby. A while later a former student of mine with her cute oppa came for a visit and said that she had gotten a divorce and been in a mental hospital. "I got divorced because my ex-oppa kept hitting me, but after the divorce I developed schizophrenia, so this time I screamed 24 hours a day as I was getting beat up by the oppa of my delusions, and I couldn't

67

sleep or eat from all the beatings." I despise pp so much. Every time I call out to pappaoppa I become ppreathless as if I'm standing in front of the ruins of Angkor Wat where the walls have crumbled and piled up on the ground. pp is even more disgusting than a burn with sprinkled black sesame seeds. pp is darkdark like a mouth closed around the two pupils of my eyes. Pappaisppadoppaisppreathless, pp is even more suffocating than kisskiss.

There is an apartment building with lights on and a tree in front of my window
At night people get sucked upp the stepps like the laundry in the washing machine
Thousands of lips hang from the apartment tree
Tens of smelly teeth hide inside each lip
Apartment tree trembles like an aspen tree and sings
Thousands of ears hang from the apartment tree
The inside of the ears is filled with screams made of smelly vowels that have turned to pus
Please don't ppull the plug of the apartment tree
What if the plug is ppulled and the sppinning laundry wet with tears falls off in droves like the leaves of the aspen tree?

oppa = older brother of a girl/woman
A strange custom has recently developed in South Korea. Women address their older boyfriends as oppa, and married women with children call their husbands papa or daddy as their children would.

68

CHEEKBIRD
따귀 새

At a bathroom of a restaurant in a foreign country
a woman was slapping a little girl's cheeks
Take it off! Take it off! The woman tried to take off the girl's wet panties
but the girl frantically resisted

Stand over there on the platform then run back here
I remembered my high school drill teacher who had slapped my cheeks
Since then I despise anyone who stands on a platform

The women's swift hand instructed the child to shut her mouth
The little girl's face twisted like a minefield hit by hail
as if salt were about to spurt out one grain at a time from her sweat
glands
It might be better to bleed than to spurt out salt
As I was washing my hands at the sink
I suddenly remembered all the hands that had landed on my cheeks
It was as if all the children who had their cheeks slapped enclosed me in
a circle

Salt gets sprinkled on
my plump chest, my warm belly
my deep navel, my sleeping rose
yet the red blood trapped inside only goes around roundroundround
It hails for three months and ten days and I get hailed on
You stole it didn't you? You hid it didn't you? The hand falling on my
cheeks
Say it! Say it! Say it! Or I'll slap you again!
Salt rolled and fell from my face

The 67-meter-high pagoda of Shanxi castle,
the oldest wooden pagoda in the world, comes to mind
Hundreds of thousands of swallows flock and encircle the giant pagoda
and they scream like pigtailed barbarians, slapping cheeks
the sound of their flapping wings are still blue 10 miles away

Outside the window trees shoot up
with red hands dangledangling from their red faces
The cheekbirds fly up between the thickly grown branches
So I was thinking that when the autumn arrives I'd send all the hands
that have slapped my cheeks to the otherworld
Shut your mouth and take off your glasses!

The pagoda leans to one side, its groin and armpits closeclosely
hammered by open-mouthed swallow chicks
The pagoda incubates a circle of seated Buddhas with caved-in faces
and bits of flesh falling from their thighs
Both the pagoda's cheeks got slapped frenziedly by hundreds of
thousands of wings
I remember how the oldest pagoda filled with the sound of the beating
filled the blue sky like a black tornado

SONGJUICE
노래주스

I can't stand the ghosts. Even if my husband says they're alright I can't stand them. When the ghosts come up through the cracks in the wooden floors my husband can pass easily through them swishswish. But I'm so busy avoiding them that I can't walk around the living room, not even to the kitchen next to it.

Every morning I plead, Dearghost dearghost please leave this house, but the dining table thumps, the fridge squeaks, the chair falls over. I really can't stand it anymore now that it's summer break.

There are six speakers in our house. Two in my husband's room, two in my daughter's, two in mine. Different songs in every room. The three doors stay shut. Each of the three rooms has different music.

Faucetghost pottedladypalmghost bluegasflameghost fridgeiceghost namelessghostghostwithaname thedaymymommygavebirthtomeghost thedayIbecameamommyghost thedayIbecameagrandmotherlongagoghost The ghosts' sighs gnaw at me as I nap. Look at this, read this, the names of the ghosts engraved on my face.

They are as demanding as a hidden lover in the attic. Perhaps the names of those that are dead and starved in death are ghosts. The green gaze of the lady palm snatches my hair pleading, Love me, love me. Those most starved for love in this world must be ghosts. A ghost on my back tells me, Get out of this house! I've never felt such a heavy wind before. When I carry a ghost on my back I weep like sad music. My thighs weep my shoulders weep my rib cage weeps. When I'm carried on the ghost's back a song plays on my speakers.

There are six speakers in our house. The ghost's song comes from my speakers. The song just plays on its own.

TEARFARMING
눈물농사

Ice princess appeared in a dream for several days running. Before long I found myself staring vacantly at the ice princess even in my waking hours. The ice princess lived somewhere over there on the snow-covered mountaintop. She lived and commanded echomaids. The echomaids didn't allow anyone to come anywhere near where they lived. When hello! came, hello!maids sent back hello! When hurrah! came, hurrah!maids sent back hurrah! When a thump! arrived, thump!maids hid the thump inside a lump of ice. Have you ever seen an ice princess with tears hanging like gigantic melted candles from her cheeks? Have you ever heard that an ice princess is tearfarming over there? When the ice princess cries a lot it's June and when she stops it's October. When the ice princess stops crying no one steps out from the mud huts, and the animals crouch down in their nests and keep chanting, ommanipadmehum ommanipadmehum. No one can get around on the road or the gravel lot. Then when June arrives the echomaids open the shed door. Then tears become a huge river and flow down a rocky mountain. People herd sheep and migrate along the flowing tears. A land shaped like a green fan appears next to the valley of the rocky mountain. Down below in the lowest desert, an oasis overflows. Then the farmers step on the teardrop-like blue barley and black dirt with their bare feet. Finally the donkeys parched in winter get to take a bath. Patchpatch of yellow rape flowers bloom on the rocky mountain. Remote mountains yellyell, a thousand fierce tearfalls hanging from them. Large animals come out of the cages and travel farfar away. As they leave, the ice princess sobs even more. She cries so hard that her hair is in danger of falling out. Her eyes form without eyelids or eyebrows and then float away. The blackest eardrums inside the whitest ears float up so high that the sky becomes dark blue. And that is when the ice princess is kicked out. Someone who ventured up near where the princess lives, frozen except for the blood in his body, returned and said that he saw the ice princess, her entire crushed body limplimp, being kicked out after she had spilled all of her whitest tears. Dark blood gushed out as the ice princess walkedwalked to dye a mound of stones black. That someone who saw the ice princess had both of his eyes put out. As I heard the princess for the first time beneath the snow-covered mountain, my mind hazed over. Even if I live for a thousand years, her wretched scream will linger in my heart. After I met her restless and painful expression, even in my waking hours, I stared at the ice princess with the icy tears streaming out of her eyes. I'm becoming so thirsty that I could drink a thousand, ten thousand buckets of ice princess' tears.

RED SUNSET
붉은 노을

1

A massive white engraving is spread out on the floor
It's Mount Everest as seen from the plane
It's as though I am flying above a painting someone has hung on the wall
After all, all the earth's mountains and seas, the fields and cities are an
engraving
No one can leave this engraving
A red hamster circles the whitetestwhite engraving all day
it must be looking for someone

2

A woman is sitting in a white bathtub, she is crying, her body breaks out
with red spots, it's no use splashing water on them or pouring cold water
into the tub, soon even the tub breaks out with red spots, the woman
becomes one with the white tub, the red flowers bloom clamclammy from
the woman's body and the tub, later the red spots pop up everywhere on
the white tiles of the bathroom

3

A young woman speaks to an old woman on the plane:
I feel like an insignificant being who lives on mere grains

fallen in between the rocks on this earth at the edge of the universe
The old woman replies:
Since the grain becomes red blood, how could it not hurt?
Terrible
The young woman also says:
Terrible
 Both say:
Terrible
Terrible

4

On the ceiling of my skull is an engraving clotted with white clouds
Try shooting with a gun at the whitestwhite engraving that floats away in
the air
Shoot at the right time like when the hands of the clock shoot
the menstruation pouch
The hamster that hid inside the engraving explodes
A red pond flows down from the top of the eyebrows of the two women
who are shooting lying down
The existence wedged between the engravings gets soaked in blood

5

The ground is ill, I won't be able to walk
The sky is ill, I won't be able to breathe either
The blood that circulates throughout my body is ill
I won't be able to live

LADY CINE
LADY CINE

What will happen to the actress
What if the theater's door is shut and the lights go off
What if she's left behind all by herself inside the film
The movie has ended but I don't get up from my seat
The actress doesn't know how to come down as if she has given her body
to the song that goes around the world
When I shout, I'm afraid!
that terrible song which begins with -id -id -id the -id of afraid starts
playing
and the actress keeps her sideways glance till late at night
like a phantom lady
and tells me the stories she has made up
What will happen to the actress if she is left all alone
locked inside the echo of the song, a place where
you can't tell whether it's yesterday or tomorrow
Now people are getting ready to leave, grabbing their umbrellas
Should she or shouldn't she go to the Seoul mouse's house
in the sewer beneath the theater
What will happen to the actress who says
I feel as if I've been hypnotized by the song
pulled by the fingertips of the hypnotist

77

as she hovers around the movie screen like this
She gets up from her bed and smokes
searing the screen with her cigarette
Bright holes light up on the screen
like the occasional streetlamps lit during the night of the waning moon
In the end she scorches her own face
The actress's phone call is received by the mommy mouse
who lives beneath the wooden floor
Mommy mouse puts down the receiver and says
All human beings will go to bed when they're done eating
Wait a bit then that woman will be ours
I wonder which movie track is playing now
as her body is trapped like something held at the pawnshop
Because the movie studio workers had the lighting too bright
crazy people pour onto the screen
but the cigarette smoke, the silver light reflector, and the director's
swearing are kept hidden
She covers her nose with her hands
but I can't tell what the smell is
If you know me, will you let me know?
She grabs a knife and tries to stab someone who is lying down next
to me
but instead she stabs me in the eye
Help me!
My call goes to the little mouse's house or to India
or to the house of the queen ant who does nothing but lay eggs every
single day
Please grab me please erase this busted dream
My punctured dream my punctured eyes the punctured night street
The toll-free call she makes burns down the room that she is calling
How did she get to be trapped inside such a whitetestwhite shell
like the shell of a boiled egg

I can't ever go outside the whitestwhite screen

THE HIMALAYAS SAID TO ME
히말라야 가라사대

Take a look at the deep-sea fish
Their feet are stuck to the bottom and stay stuck their entire lives
For them, being born means sinking deep down
all the way to the bottom, falling for a lifetime

Take a look at the deep-sea fish
Look at their bodies stuck to the bottom like an engraved print
They are dark, not a single drop of light leaks from them
Look at those dark lumps, lumped by loneliness
The water pressure must be horrendous
The woman comes up carrying a knapsack
her panting lips stay parted

Take a look, I've lost my ring in the abyss
A meteor falls and hits the ocean
My snow flurries can never reach the inside of the deep, deep water
My heart that has floated above the surface flutters
They say that something that has once flowed away never returns

80

Take a look, below the horizon far away
The woman carrying a knapsack comes up
Red sunset, waves of blood on the painting woman's
white pants splash about inside and outside of her
The feet of the deep-sea fish only get unstuck from the bottom when they
die

ALCHEMY
연금술

Let's pour the moonlight that flowflows down in front of me
into the cast iron pot and simmer it like taffy
Then let's carry the thing hardened to a rock to your door and test it
to see if it is a metal bit that fits perfectly into the hole of your lock

Let's lift up the mountain ranges that have run in streamstreams towards
my eyes
and take them to the blacksmith shop and temper them for several days
Then let's take that thing that has shrunk to the size of a pinkie to your
door
and test it to see if it is a ridge that fits perfectly into the hole of your lock

Don't just cry while you hammer a rusted nail
bangbang into the ground in front of the gate of Ssangkye Temple
instead let's stare at the key-like crescent moon
that has supposedly been simmering in sunlight for millions of years

CAT
고양이

interesting

As I'm taking my socks off before bed
the rats that my paws have stepped on today
run towards me from far over there
then the fattened rats
ask me to eat them, eat them
I am so full that I can barely breathe
but they say I can fall asleep only if I eat them all
The skinny god holding a whip sits and waits on the bed
I asked god, Please grant me divine soul, a flame
that splits like a tongue!
He sent me an army of rats with ponytails
Already there are many, many rats living inside me, yet
I even have many baby rats that have just popped out
from mommy rats' stomachs and they'll grow into mommies by tomorrow,
yet mommies' stomachs are bulging from second third fourth generations
of rats
Mommy rats even eat their baby rats while in labor, yet
I'm told to eat, eat again
Hordes of rats are filling up my whole body till I'm ready to burst
Really, I'm heavier than a pine tree dangling pinecones
Where did you place your filthy paws today?

83

Where have you been all day?
I've finished pounding rice
and I filled the bottomless jar with water, yet
I'm told that I'm late, I'm late, I must swallow the pack of black rats
Rat! Sin! Rat! Sin! Rat! Sin! The whip keeps lashing down on my head
I want to become a pine tree that falls on the bed, thump!
But I'm still awake with eyes open like two triangles
and I keep swallowing one rat, two rats
The world has eaten up all of its prey
but I still tear my body open then glue it back together
as I eat three rats, four rats till dawn

LOULAN KINGDOM
누란

A country that nobody remembers or talks about
A country that no one is curious about, whose old name no one
remembers
There was such a country
A country with no yesterday or tomorrow   *→ liminal/ present*
like an old high school friend no one remembers anymore
because she grew up an orphan, married early, and died
even before she could give birth to a baby
I said that such a country used to exist in Asia
to a woman poet I met from a foreign country
who then made a big deal out of the snow falling from the sky
and said to me, Then you must be seeing snow for the first time
So I joked, That country was covered in snow and disappeared!
No one was left after the snow melted!
Then the blue-eyed woman who thought that there was no winter in Asia
said, Then it can't be Asia!
A country that disappeared like a snowflake melting on the tip of the
tongue
like a strand of grey hair that dangled from the beloved's shoulder
Nobody remembers this country even when it disappears before a child
grows to adulthood

Being born in that country is a good idea if you are the kind of person who wants to vanish after staying briefly inside the eyes of an owl and a luminous jellyfish

The people of that country don't even trust what they see with their own eyes

Poet Yi Sang, who had put the country on his doorsill to look at in winter must have burnt it with his magnifying glass

that's why it can't be found when you put it on a table under the microscope, and even when you look for it holding a lantern there's not even a door to pound on bangbangbang

The people who used to get up in the morning and shake their blankets and swarm outside into the sunlight, where did they all go? They don't return even when you wait for them with lights brightly lit at night with food on the table

A country that can never be found

When you send a letter it gets returned with REFUSED stamped on it

A country that doesn't flinch even when you threaten it, You're really going to be that way, even if I die?

Now I am even starting to doubt whether such a country ever existed

No one speaks about the birth and the death of that country

like an unknown race that lived deep under the sea then disappeared

A country as harsh as that hides on the backside of a map

MAPA
에미애비

The day when even the tongue inside my mouth feels cumbersome
The day when even my toes and toenails are nauseating
The day when I play by myself smelling the smell of my body
I think of the day when I'll discard my body

The elders of Varanasi stare out as if they are thirsty
at the flames of the cremation site
across the river
The elders rent a room next to the cremation site
They have money in their pockets for the firewood for their cremation
They can't spend their money, they have to starve again today

Our body is like a tunnel, so it can't be shared with anyone
At the end over there
only the red tongue awaits us
The smell of burning protein hovers briefly in the air

The elders of Tibet practice
Every day they recite the multiplication table of the netherworld
When Death arrives to take them away
they ride on the sharp straight light
and get on top of Ma's strong new womb

87

The old man at the Samye Monastery's sky burial site
wets his lips and stares at the eagles
He looks up at the lama's whitestwhite apron as if it were a white cloud
He stares at the lama's axe with the solemn eyes of a live fish on the
cutting board
at a Japanese restaurant as if the axe were a chef's knife that would
make a meal out of his body
The elders beg for food next to the sky burial site

Oh Dear Butcher! This chunk of meat!
These smelly tears of butter!
As the lama brings the axe down
blood splatters onto his apron

Children only call their MaPa when they are clinging onto their Ma's
breasts
Children grow up and cut, burn, smash their MaPa

Terrible and gruesome fuck!
Fuck-like tunnel!
My body that is persistently solitary like the tunnel beneath my feet!
A body that is a smelly lump of protein lying atop the cutting board!

RAINY SEASON
장마

The ghosts always gripegripe
The women who met an undeserved death are the noisiest among them
A crazy ghost unexpectedly comes dripdrip quietly
A female ghost who has fallen for her first love comes somewhat fiercely
for the lightning attaches itself to her hair

Don't pound on the lake too hard
Blood water surges out of all the places where you pound

That woman who has worms coming out of her mouth
please don't hit her too hard
One sack, two sacks of worms fall out of her mouth
because she gets beaten every single day
Later she even pukepukes out her intestines
and her empty body gets mashed
Oh the stench

Have you ever had a bad encounter with a ghost that died in the forest?
The ghost pulls out from its mouth vines that stretch endlessly
and blue tongues dangdangle from the vines
and those tongues chatter all night long
the ghosts are so tirelessly noisy
they leave then return
they come looking for you even when you chase them away
They gripegripe and their sweat splatters over heaven and earth
like the smoke that fills the house on a memorial day

The lake has opened thousands of its mouths and begins to chatter
Who will plug up those red mouths now?
Oh all of heaven and earth is a lake, it's red

90

EVERYTHING IS RICE
모두 밥

A knife blade is raised high
and a softsoft body
is cut up on top of me
Fresh flesh is thinly sliced on top of me
Blood spreads over my skin
and countless cuts are made but I don't die, so I trembletremble
like an old man who sunbathes when the sun comes out
and windbathes when the wind blows
Like a girl who has left home and washes away her tears in rainwater
I rinse off the blood
like rinsing a cutting board

All the raised arms resemble flames
so does the wood, the surrender, and the victory cheer
I hang the pots on the wrists of the flame tree
and cook rice and boil soup
When I go to school all the students have taken off
I open up the attendance book on my empty desk
and stuffstuff myself and scald the ceiling of my mouth
for they say no eat no gain
In my hand I bunch up the faces that glimmer before my eyes

and knead them vigorously and make a dumpling soup
like a rice pot that knows nothing

That was many years ago
but my kitchen is still filled with the same things
Hell's vigor covers the cutting board
and the smell of the ghosts floats about the rice pot
I have even thought to myself,
I wish all the kitchens in the world would disappear
Those were the days when
the cutting boards grew in the mountains instead of trees
and lumps of dough were born instead of students in the classroom

(Please don't speak about those days, turn down the volume)

LIKE THE HAND THAT BREAKS THE HEART
가슴을 에는 손길처럼

Maybe they're leaves that have fallen from *shindansu* in autumn
Two leaves for each of the ten million people of Seoul, so twenty million
leaves rustle
They rustle nonstop, not pausing even for a second, trying to reattach
themselves to something ✳

A traditional military band goes up the street of falling leaves
Two hands and ten red fingers on a trumpet wiggle nonstop
as if they are trying to reattach themselves to something

When the discarded things make contact they clasp and even shake
each other
but when the veins of the leaves touch each other they are startled by
how easily they crumble and fall off

The discarded things!
They flutter about not knowing where they are supposed to go like the two
rats under the scorching sun!
The poverty one is born into has to be on the move constantly
At some point they'll throw down their trumpets and get carried off by
the wind!

93

A dismal fate!

The dreary autumn wind blows and as the two leaves that stick
to the end of my sleeves curl up
I lose the bundle I'm carrying and get slapped on the cheeks by the wind

Your five fingers lie on the bed like pitiful hooks
Like a rat I gnawgnaw your hand that breaks the heart

When night comes Mr. Janitor carts off two sacks of hands he has swept
up by day
The two leaves that push the cart away grow distant

In the Korean creation myth, *shindansu* is the first tree that
came down from the sky.

94

SEA JELLY
바다 젤리

Mommy, jelly from different regions from different countries all taste
different
The jelly sold at a café at the Pompidou Center is sour
the jelly sold in front of the Forbidden City is crumbly
and is coated so thickly with sugar
The jelly I ate in Seoul was as tough as plastic

Mommy, it feels as though my time here is like cold jelly
It's sweet, then cold at times, I slowly pass through the inside of the jelly

I go to my parent's house next to the East Sea
park my car by the beach and look down
The night sea is jelly
I can't help thinking that
the sea surrounds the three sides of our country, a peninsula
like the lubricant that surrounds the wall of a uterus
I suffer from indigestion all the time
so I spitspit towards the night sea
and wonder why all the things that come out of the human body are
sticky

95

Soon I see a shaman I know going down the cliff with a white paper boat
in her hands to set it afloat on the sea for a ritual, to rescue a departed
spirit

As the moon rises against the wall of the uterus like an infant's head
the moonlight gushes out like a placenta, sticky by the night sea
The shaman comes back up the cliff, waving the flagpole
she must have rescued the spirit in the sea
The rescued spirit tastes soursour like a nameless green jelly

Yes, time must be something sticky that comes out of the human body
Mommy tastes like something I want to vomit as if I'd eaten asphalt!
The silence in the plaza in front of a city hall at five in the morning in the
rain!
That taste!
I write back to my daughter

SCREAMLIFE
비명생명

Mr. Scream, my life's guide
Thanks to you I still stand upright
When you burn fiercely I grow brighter
When you burn fiercely a passerby turns around to look at me
My body is midday, leaked from night   *excess*
or it may be insomnia worse than a dream
Tonight I send my regards to you, an electrical current
Hello Mr. Scream!
I'll feed you my daily anguish every day

I never know how to leave you
I don't know the way

A frog charged with your electricity croaks all night
The charged stems of silver grass
flare up in white-gold
The grasshoppers that spatter flames with their mouths
gnaw away at the crop in the rice paddy

As if I am riding on a whale that is gasping for air
the lightening sky trembles
and my skirt charged with electricity
opens like a parachute
Everyone will be able to see me
even if I fly far away

I wouldn't be able to look outside my body   *outside/*
                                              inside
if it weren't for the bundle of screams inside me
I wouldn't be able to say what I've just said
While you pull up the water column from my insides like a water fountain
and make it stand like this and drag me around
I would most likely stay alive with my eyes gleaming

My beloved Mr. Scream, a hundred-watt bulb lights up inside my mouth
then I swallow the anguish-filled scream ahahah till the night explodes
ahahah I still don't know how to let you out
so I convulse like a winter tree charged by electricity in a pitch dark night

98

CINDERELLA
신데렐라

Our city is made of ice
An ice carriage slides on the ice pavement
Ice horses' manes stand up and glitter
Ice coachman skillfully wields the ice whip
Today is the day of the dancing ball
the ice bell rings from the ice palace
the ice chandelier descends like angels' toes

The trees are surrounded by the bluestblue sparkling ice
My beloved iceman dances trapped in ice then leaves
Our ice flesh mingled, loved, gave birth, and danced

The world we created is as blue as the infant's funeral march
People's gazes are blind and clean as if made from ice dew

Take a look around my world made of cold like the inside of a transformer
In the quiet ice room of the winter fish water boils in the ice teapot
No one can enter here but you and I

But the moment we are caught off guard
stepmothers' cold toenails dig into our flesh like icicles
The netherworld pretends to love us so much
It may be keeping us fresh only to pull the plug later
When we get slapped by a hand as hot as lead
our blood rots and our bodies fall like timber
In that world we can only pass through each other's bodies
like two converging cold winds

For us there is no future
only our vivid faces sealed in the ice
In our bosom the North Pole and South Pole happily embrace
and my ice slipper falls down the steps and freezes

But now it is time to return, the ice rooster lets out a long crow
I really don't want to go there where tears endlessly gush from my body
That place where the red flower has blossomed is where my heart was
sewn
I never want to see that filthy place again

I killed the ice rooster all night long, Stop crowing! I gagged it
I plucked white feathers and threw them into the air
But now it is time to offer the whitest ice rooster to the ice palace and
return

Heartless time drank the last glass of wine on the table
The last piece of ice glittered in your hand

The carriage speeds away and cries pour out like a snowstorm
Ice shoes melt, ice carriage melts
only the coachman holding a whip is left
The coachman asks, Damn it, why won't you stop crying?

BRIGHT ROOMS
환한 방들

The copy machine vomits out
sunflowers every second
No sooner do I turn around than
the room is filled with sunflower blossoms
All the flowers of the sunflower patch have copied
the sun so diligently that every one of their heads is bent
as if the ageless Sophia
were about to step out from the garden

My copy machine, every time I enter this square, bright box
it scattscatters the black bouquet of flowers that it has kept in its heart
into the air and smiles like the excavated mummy at Tutankhamen's
pyramid
This is the room where the lips live, the lips I need to feed and make laugh
my bright room where the breeze and sighs go in and out incessantly!

Every time the copy machine lights up every second
and pushes and pulls my body
the inhaling breath goes in and the exhaling breath comes out

inside/
outside

101

My face that has been copied onto thin paper
sits on the long seat of the subway train, line number 4
and falls into the faint light for the millionth time
My face doesn't even know where its original is
I have already become as faint as faint can be
I draw the route of my next commute

When I return home, I wash my face with a soap named Despise
and erase my face with a face cream called Deface
I who have been photocopied tonight
tear up my spiral notebook that got filed away
Do I ultimately live inside my body?
When I turn off the light switch in the bright room
where my final, barely photocopied smile stays afloat
the square copy machine box goes dark
and my body also grows dark as the inside of a coffin

MOON

달

She is an expert tightrope walker
When I say I would like some tea
she walks along the tightrope and brings tea rattling the cup and saucer
When I say, It's time to eat
she walks along the tightrope and carries a table with food
precariousprecariously
When I say, There are many other paths besides this
she hangs upside down from the rope in the air and is covered by her
skirt
as if she were swinging from a parallel bar
and says, Sister, don't say such a thing. This rope is round.
Once you are hooked by the circle there is no exit from it.
The moon's eyelashes flutterflutter rise fall like a camel's
Perhaps her ceiling is leaking, for one or two
water droplets dangle from the ceiling
and even when the floor stays soaked in water
she turns and turns around the same orbit
like a pearl dangling from a necklace
Her yellow coffee-spill and stew-spill stains
have spread on her floor like trodden petals
The vase with withered flowers smells of the graveyard

103

She has woken up from her sleep on the rope
one of her cheeks is always swollen

PINKBOX
핑크박스

Pinkbox that has just arrived. Pinkbox that waits to be opened. When I embrace the box, it smells of a faraway place. But no one who goes inside can escape. Ah adorable pinkbox. Pinkbox, my first baby. Hello, pinkbox. I want to rock pinkbox in a cradle. (For your information, God doesn't know how to make anything rectangular.)

Folded pinkbox. I want to forget about everyone. Want to forget about Mommy and Daddy. I'll just lie down like a knife blade and dream only of revenge. Pinkbox has two hidden breasts that pull on the chest painfully. Blood streamed down pinkbox. This box is smaller than me. It's unbearably tight. Pinkbox has a bleeding pinkhole. Pinkbox will die if the tape is ripped and light is shone inside. I'm a sick pinkbox. I hated the pink all the time. It's useless to try and be heard outside the box. No one listens closely to what a box has to say. Rest, eat, forget, bell ringing box. Pinkbox can't speak, hear, or see under the deafdeaf blackboard. You need to become a sick pinkbox if you don't want to go to school. Look over there at the high-rise apartment building. In each box boxes lean and look out at the same boxes.

Dented pinkbox. Love has been a prisoner inside me since I was born. Someone gnawed at pinkbox like a cornered rat every time I couldn't see you. Pinkbox is still a pinkbox no matter how many times it gets folded. Pointless to ask pinkbox what's in the box. I'll become a pinkbox that sings, drifts about, and overflows when you arrive. I'll become a boat with a pink light, foaming its way through the rainy night. I'll become a boat of pink light carrying trees with leaves out to the widewide sea. Yet, life is nothing but a glance from a torn hole, a distant thing. I'm just an empty box, a discarded, crushed pinkbox.

Unfolded pinkbox. Has spit out all the precious writing like an old silkworm. When did this all happen? Like a lone plank of wood floating in the sea of pitch-black darkness. There's nothing. Pinkbox takes a lashing from the rain. Dirty toes dig in as pinkbox gets flattened in the underground passage. Pinkbox with cold hands and feet. When will I sink down?

Fallen pinkbox. Torn pinkbox, pinkbox cast away, it might be better to grab onto the horizon. Can't embrace it since it has parted far. *Dirty pinkbox, smelly pinkbox, crumpled pinkbox, flowing pinkbox.* Pinkbox covered with faded writing, dirty pink, old pink, open hole pink, flapping, its hair down pink. Like a camera, pink captures you, but there is nothing after the film is taken out. Don't let the box return. It's just dirty paper. Burn this box.

THE STONES "DO"
돌이 '하다'

Who says that someone leaves and someone arrives?

The valley beneath the scorching sun is filled with pebbles

It's filled with tightly closed fists that can't go anywhere

On the wall reliefs at the temple of the west the stones "do"

They make music and wage war with their backs stuck to the stonewall

When my gaze touches them, they bury the backs of their heads in the stonewall and make love as if for the first time

The stones are "doing" for the thousandth year

They don't even have any hair in their armpits, but they are "doing" it

But who says that someone has left and someone will arrive?

Can I turn to stone if I clench my fists and teeth?

Will my eyeballs that open to the outside also turn to stone?

107

If I clench my fists will the dawn never unfold?

I pick up a pebble and clench it

The pebble becomes wet like a meteor that has fallen after flickering for a while soaked in dark blood

A handful of pebbles plunge down inside me like a million-ton's worth of anesthesia
Will I turn into stone standing like this?

I came this far but didn't go anywhere

I put my toe in the spot where I picked up the pebble

It feels as warm as though my foot were deep inside someone's ribs

Who says what is arriving and what is leaving?

How terrible the smell of the rotting stone is!

THE FISHBOWL INSIDE MY TUMMY IS SO AWKWARD
뱃속의 어항은 정말 처지 곤란이야

In *Eternity and a Day* Bruno Ganz said that
the pebbles that we play with are time

When I asked, Would I be able to make a fishbowl inside my tummy if I
kept swallowing those pebbles? the youngest woman amongst us spoke:

When I was very little, my mommy was busy. We only saw each other
when we ate breakfast, so she unloaded the whole day's nagging all at
once at the dining table as she whackwhacked my head with her spoon,
so I scooped up a spoonful of rice and swallowed the pebbles hidden in it.
The pebbles only went down when I swallowed them with my tears. When
I didn't, they kept lumping up in my throat. Then another woman spoke:

To make a fishbowl inside your tummy, you have to swallow live goldfish,
and that's really difficult to do. Every time I had to put up with an unfair
evaluation, I swallowed a goldfish flapping about in my spoon. When I
made rice and veggies for him at midnight, he whacked my head with a
spoon, and the rice became alive. Every time I lifted up my spoon, each
grain of rice flapped about, so I had to eat with my eyes closed. Really,
it's more difficult to swallow live things than pebbles. The fishbowl inside

my tummy is half fish and half tears. Would you like to cut it up and take some with you? Then the oldest woman amongst us spoke:

What's even more difficult is throwing away the fishbowl. I wanted to discard the fishbowl and leave this country to go somewhere far off, so I called up this and that person and offered them my fishbowl, but nobody wanted it. In fact, I even went to this and that café holding the fishbowl in my arms and asked if they might want it for decoration. I just couldn't empty the bowl in the street or into the river.

After watching the boring movie, we, the three women, didn't know what to do with the fishbowls in our tummies

We held our sloshsloshing bloated bellies and walked down the streets of Chongno

ALL THE STORIES OF THE WORLD
세상의 모든 이야기

It's forbidden to call anyone by their names in that house! Instead
you can say Daddymommybigbrotherlittlesiblings. We all get startled
when someone asks, *What's your mom's name?* Grandmother was
the first one to disappear from the house. Her mind frequently left the
house, then eventually her body failed to return. Next my younger
sister disappeared. She rolled up her blankets into a ball then vanished
without a trace. Daddymommyuncle looked everywhere for my sister,
but she was nowhere to be found, not even at the top of the ceiling
or the transmission tower. We installed an antenna high on the roof,
hoping we could meet her in our dreams, but we never saw her again.
Daddymommyuncle's lips became chapped from the stress of my sister's
disappearance. Next Uncle vanished into the water. He left a note, but
it was so abstract that no one could understand it. Then it was Daddy.
All he did was drink after my younger sister had disappeared, then
he vanished without a word. It was pointless to scream or cover your
ears. Mommy didn't cry at all. People pointed their fingers at the house
and said it was haunted. Who do you think will be next? My younger
brother took off on a motorcycle and disappeared. *Please make the
disappearances dis ap pear.* Mommy unthreaded herself and knitted
scarves again and again but eventually she disappeared into the scarves.
Maybe Daddymommybigbrotherlittlesiblings is a nifty nickname for people

who will soon disappear. Anyhow everyone disappeared forever in that house except for Daddymommybigbrotherlittlesiblings. That's because the child became an aunt, and the virgin became a new bride, and the reader became the writer. And because Stepmomstepdadstepunclestepsister were born with new scarves around their necks. For generations, it has been forbidden to call anyone by their names in that house! In the forest the trees that will be cut for Daddymommyunclesister's coffins are growing zealously. The lumber mill planed the trees with zealzeal zealzeal. And long long ago there lived a big brother and his pretty younger sister, and the writers leaned over their desks and tirelessly wrote the same stories.

MY THROAT HAS BECOME A CANDLESTICK
목구멍이 촛대가 되었네요

When I lie and wait at the riverside it's my turn again, the river cleans my body, the heedless wind blows in and makes my white sleeves flutter, my tears dry up, you have washed your hair and have a white towel wrapped around your neck, you lift me up to the bed of flames, you pour butter down my throat and place a wick in it, you light the wick, my throat has become a candlestick, my organs burn up like beeswax, green flames shoot out from my mouth, outside the bed my feet shout, It's cold it's cold, you cover my chest with a layer of straw, you set fire to the straw, you sprinkle petals on me as though you occasionally think of me, you even throw incense sticks at me, as you ignite the floor's radiant heat I spit fire from my whole body, my ribs are burning, my muscles dance like when a scarecrow is thrown onto the bonfire, in the middle of the blaze I cry and scream and also suddenly stand up, I give birth to my death, I curl up, I'm in labor delivering death, when I'm done I even watch my burning naked body, the blaze escorts death to the wind, you scatter the ash by the river, you also take a handful of ash and taste it, I who have turned into ash don't taste good, I have no thought, now the ash no longer belongs anywhere in the world—sky, earth, and air, the ash make up a sack, two sacks, goodness, ten sacks, you keep staring at the river even when a mangy dog takes off with my eyeball that has become as big as the sky, you wash off the remainder of the ash with the water in the washbowl. Then you go down to the river to wash the ash from your body,

113

why do you poke at my thigh with a skewer?
why do you beat down on my head?
so you'll burn well

BATHROOM
화장실

The house is so high up!
It can receive the saliva of the night sky
that growls like a wolf that hates Seoul
I wake up in the middle of the night
and head straight to the bathroom
and open wide my crescent-moon-like eyes
hidden behind a black cloud
Naturally, I head to the bathroom high up in the air

Today is the day my new book of poems is coming out
My poems have sucked the life out of me my whole life
I wish I could pull down a lever and scatter the poems
back to the place where they came from
a place that swarms with nameless things

Like a lost wolf in the forest
I want to receive the rage the clouds spew out
Come down from the highesthigh sky
I want my neck to be hit by the frozen saliva

Where did the tears that I shed last night before I fell asleep go?
Where did the rainwater that once enveloped my whole body go?
Where did the aches that sent shocks to the end of my toenails every
night go?
Down there water tanks sit on every roof submerged in thought like
sealed wells

I hang on to Seoul's cliff and wash myself
I also want to wash the inside of my body clean with a brush

The bathroom trembletrembles the day my book comes out
the pipes inside the concrete trembletremble along
and the name of the named is still dirty

As I come out all clean
my tongue that has not yet learned to speak
is stuck outside on the balcony's window
drooldrool drooling
as though it has kept sad words from me its entire life

116

MANHOLE HUMANITY
맨홀 인류

O

Goodness, I didn't know there were such repulsive holes!

My hairy holes!
Creases of my stomach
Hair-like cilia in my nostrils
Finger-like villi in my small intestine
Pubic hair of love
Hair sprouts up inside the holes and ripples like water plants.
Holes are neatneatly piled inside a steaming stomach.
The wet and most poisonous snakes in the world pant.
Fill us up! Fill us up with the outside!
Delicious outside!
When hair whines like the fingers that reach out towards the refugee-aid
bread truck someone picks up a brass instrument and wails at the sky
praising the blueness.
Holes of the world, open up your lids and howl!

117

O

Bile travels up the esophagus and collects in my mouth. My esophagus feels as if it's burning. The drain regurgitates. It's potent. It's as if ceiling and floor are stuck together. Right now I'm being thrashed about by a whip made of horizontal lines. In my dream someone comes into my room to surf.

In my dream I burn like a charcoal briquette, a wick placed down in my neck. In the next dream, I become a gas in the dream world of gases. I hear wind in my ears.

I dream of my holes falling onto a cement floor. I clean them up with a plastic brush.

A faucet leaks. Water starts to collect in the basement. My pillow floats above the basement.

Look over this way! As I open my eyes, the doctor pokes my tear glands with a long needle. Tears collect in my mouth. They're salty. I stare at the ocean inside me.

Nerve holes of a neck become constricted and put pressure on the entire nerve tree. A tranquilizer is injected directly into the holes. It is given six times a day. The piano keeps shut its gum that is about to spew out blood.   *disconnect*

My right shoulder hurts, but the doctor inserts a needle in my left toe. With a stick, the doctor explains the swirls of my holes and the structure of my spirals. Someone sticks his head outside my manhole and looks out. Someone screams from my throat.

118

My body covered with holes wants to escape leaving the holes behind.

Nausea comes up the hole. As I take off my skin, the pipes holed in my body leak.

A lit stethoscope moves through the pipe. A night bus dashes along the endless roads inside my body. The night bus flickers like pain.

O

Hole, the heart of all things.
Hole, my country, my matter, my toasty-warm god.
Hole, stay eternal! All things endure a life of nuisance through small uteruses then die for the sake of the eternal life of a big uterus. Dear queen ant's many uteruses packed inside that high mountain: my eating and breathing has to do with my worship of the hole. This is my lifelong commemorative hole rite. Please get up, Your Highness, it's morning. Here is a fresh cup of coffee. Please calm down, Your Highness, it's nighttime. Here is a glass of wine for your fluttering brain. When he made me by blowing his breath into a hole, he who has created the world by drilling a hole into misery, the stink of his breath was overwhelming; today, I want to make him starve.

Wind, please stroke the alveoli of my lungs as you would a sick child. Please relay the message that time's pimp has not died; it still lives here. Please relay the message that the hole remains eternal from its previous life to its next life. Please relay the message that the hole gives birth to a hole and is raising a hole. (But who else is listening to what I'm saying besides my hole?)

reproduction +
time

119

O

All together: Dear Hole has died
            Dear Hole has resurrected
            Dear Hole lives again

(Holes eat and drink)

O

At midnight, the kids, still wet behind the ears, head to head with
the hole's entrance inside the subway are screaming, swallowing,
tremtremtrembling, and barking that the entire subway spurts up like
fountain water, smelling fishy.

Inside the subway station, a child holds out his dirty hands.
He says he will be good. He says he won't be bad again.
I see the child at the station for several weeks.

At the hospital across the street, a hole is giving birth to a hole.
Please allow the safe delivery of a hole!
As a mother hole of a mother hole prays rubbing her two palms together,
a soprano climbs up an organ made of hospital drainpipes in the delivery
room, panting, then lets out a scream towards the sky. Dear Big Hole,
please spit it out! This hole can't possibly handle a newborn. Please spit
it out, Dear Big Hole! (Who decides the time of birth? Is it the baby? the
Mommy? the Stars?)

A life sprouts from the fugue raging in the hallway of the hospital. It's
nearly midnight.

Another manhole humanity is born. Time makes a hole in the baby's body.

Time puts a manhole's lid on the baby's head.

Down below at the restaurant, the chef's hands are in motion! With both hands he hacks away at the bodies piled up on the cutting board; there is nothing to distinguish one from another—plants and animals, jealousy, solitude, and spirit.

When I eat them tomorrow morning, does it mean that I will be eating my hole's skin? Eating my hole's outside? Eating my hole's tether? My hole's desire to persist, the music performed by commas has no pauses, hurhurrah!

O

The hole's essence is such that it's empty like the empty space inside of a flame.
Tongue is that place, not wearing any underwear, it hangs onto the hole's end where there is nothing and licks and makes o o o sounds.

Therefore, to say regulate your desire means to regulate well the empty space, the inside of a blood sausage!
Goodness, how am I suppose to regulate a place that's invisible!
The factory supervisor who sits inside the hungry sausage—what does he look like?

O

At the intensive care unit, one floor below the gynecology ward,
an electrical cord is plugged into a hole, a graph chart rotates waahwaah,
the heart beats bambam, then later the hole dies. Time of death: 12
minutes past midnight. One handless watch stops.
The watch burns when the holes of the dead sag from greeting happiness

for the first time.
Skin remains and is placed in the drawer of a freezer and a hole filled with happiness floats in air.

O

Dark tunnel before death
White tunnel after death

O

What nonsense, you say? Love comes out from where, you ask?
How can love come out from this hole then go into that hole, you ask?
Clear away the smelly hole, you ask?

O

Mommy manhole pats a baby manhole as if she's tapping on the stovepipe.
What a strange manhole!
It even has two holes from which tears gush out waah waah waah whenever it's hungry.
Its two nostril-chimneys wail chugchugpuffpuff.
Every time the baby manhole cries, mommy manhole plays a bandoneon, stretching then pressing, her tango musician hands in motion!

After the pipe connecting to the baby manhole was cut, it caused complications in mommy hole's blood circulation and made her break out in blue rashes, so she had to go down to the lower level of the hospital to repair her hole.

Baby is this hole
Mommy is that hole

Like the swimmers who each swim in separate lanes
the holes across are all different places.

O

Washbowls and bedpans on hospital beds make loud noises
and the inside of the mattresses fill up with reddish abdominal fluids.
Fluorescent lights with lots of dead flies inside their casings bleach empty
corridors blue and nurses throw into the sewer things the damaged holes
have vomited.
Manholes with hats on them that look like white clouds!
There is a rumor that those holes carry a drug-resistant strain of blood-
poisoning virus.

O

Try relaxing your legs and raising your hands above your head
to attain the posture of the rising steam.
Imagine that all the holes of your body are opening.
Think of your solid body changing to a liquid body and then to a gas body.
Unwind the additions, multiplications of your holes.
Try and picture your body whirling down the drain.
Then imagine the blue sky sitting on the holes, relieving itself!

My legs and arms dangle all over from the big drainpipe
and a heavy manhole lid is on top of my neck!

A girl is crying in her sleep, for she took a wrong step and fell into a hole.
The girl crawls into the deepest part of a cave.
A headlamp lights up a ravine between my body and soul
like a mole digging into dark earth.
I'm looking for the girl. Like a snail she crawls under a huge rock.

123

IV solution drops plopplop, trying to make a hole in my cave.
A lit mirror passes by glancing at my one-floor body.
Here, at times as one, insects, reptiles, rodents, mists, galaxies with wasted nerves
surge upwards as monsters, but today for some reason only the girl's cry can be heard.

Look here, says the doctor
The hole's joint is constricted

What kind of melody from the hole is the EKG's machine connected to?
What kind of melody from the hole is the lie detector connected to?

O

Black smoke rises from the hole. It's the smoke from my own burning.
I shoot up! Up! A black maze, the unending spiral that begins at my feet.
The black smoke that has traveled through the hidden rooms inside the maze wails, thundering beneath the clogged sky.

My face, my hair swirl and get sucked into my hole.
I get sucked down the storm drain.
At that moment, I try to remember who it was that sat in each dirty room that was plunging down!
Do I hear the quivering sound of calling that room from this room? Do I hear myself calling me from the outside?
Who is that person getting soaked in black rain, hanging onto a thin rope above a bottomless abyss?

Why does my sleep that is solely mine return at last from elsewhere?
Why does my love that is solely mine return at last from elsewhere?
Why does my misery that is solely mine return at last from elsewhere?

124

Misery, where did you come from?
What what did you burn and run back like this?
Are you me? Who's this?
Why is a train living inside a hole?
Am I being derailed by the train along with the rhythm of it saying Love
You Love You?
The train that has taken all those many passengers to death!
A tunnel goes around inside the dark mountain and the train passes by
me like a storm.

Should I starve the train to death?

O

Love that is about a hole, a hole for the benefit of a hole, according to
a hole. I use the hole as I pretend to talk about love. I use the hole as I
pretend to talk about sadness. I use the hole as I pretend to talk about
you. I use the hole as I pretend to talk about myself. I use the writing of
the hole, the hole according to the hole, for the benefit of the hole. I stop
and look into my body. It's a mask that surrounds the hole. The rise and
fall of civilization leaves a pattern on the mask then disappears. When the
mask is ripped up, there is no hole. I try walking. All kinds of grotesque
structures around the architecture of the hole walk rattlerattle. I walk
holding up my neck stiffstiff, not even stepping with two hands on the
ground like a cow or a bitch. I'm a mixture, an upright sound, that gets
poured into the mold that is "nothing." I'm a weak structure into which
anxiety can easily intrude. Finally, I bow daily to victorious "nothing"! My
flesh! In India people greet each other as the "god inside you" by saying
Namaste. Who is pulling the trigger attached to my body just replicated
from the mold?

125

This hole is structured in such a way that its exit sucks in its entrance. Death is designed to suck in birth. It was widely known that one of the princes of the Chosôn Period was born without an exit. Because it was against the law to make a hole in the prince's body, he died. Inside the hole's structure, my time gets excreted nonstop. I am swallowed by the hole then get excreted as a hole.

O

One side of the first apple bursts and gets sucked through the lips of the naked first woman. The original woman's yellow teeth and smelly tongue begin to grind the apple into small bits. Cold wind, suns, apple blossoms, the gentle strokes of rain on my cheeks all get sucked into a wormhole. The apple doesn't know where it's going, but it follows the general theory of relativity and gets swept down a funnel. A legend spreads, that time-travel becomes possible if you go through the funnel. A legend spreads, that if you leave here and arrive in the distant past and kill the lethal snake, I will get to stay in the vast spaciousness, the time of being unborn. In order to digest this hole, an adequate amount of yin mass is needed. Digestive juices are quickly produced inside the hole.

Empty my hole. Amylase enzyme. Vesta digestive aid. The hole secretes digestive juices and mixes them with whatever it sends down. After it ingests the apple, the pitiful hole gulps for more towards the emptiness. It flails about like a snake that has fallen into the sea.

O

Hole is the prostitute of sky world
Hole is the second wife of emptiness
Hole is the prostitution cave of time
Hole is the scout of sleep
Hole is the soldier of farewell

126

The hole's architecture has no floors. So it's the deepest in the world.
There is no one who can fill the hole's architecture.
I get sucked into the deep hole of oblivion, like when a little pianist in front
of a piano suddenly gazes into the universe of music and glances around
the galaxy's scarf, like when the rain that falls on a coastal city doesn't
get to live even for a few minutes on earth but swirls down the drain and
reaches the sea in an instant. I become distant and distant again. "I cry
out to you, Lord, from a deep place!" (Shout twice)

O

At one point a rumor spread that, if you can digest all the rats living in the
hole, you could reach nirvana and wouldn't ever have to be born again.
An afternoon of a woman already pregnant with the next life walking
waddlewaddling by. Packs of rats are bartering me in my hole. I hear a
chorus of rapid breathing.

Do you know that as you walk into the backlight, you are a hole floating in
air? I who walk you am another hole? The inside of your hole is infinite?

O

Sometimes, a woman living in a hole can pop out from it.
A deep-sea woman hasn't been exposed to light before. She's a red
skinless monster.
She has a round face, exhausted by the whirling of time.
Her heart is hanging from a street lamp, so sometimes an entire alley can
echo boomboom.
Sometimes my blood becomes cold and my shadow and I swap bodies.
There are no holes in a shadow. Shadow is an afterlife.

O

I get on an elevator and press the button for basement parking. As I leave the hospital, my hole writes. It writes with a fine point, dark henna ink flowing out from it. A dream scooped up by the hole's abyss writes. A woman in the hole stretches her arms and legs outside the hole and writes. She makes the hole cry and shrieking words pour out from her. Her tongue jumbles them up. But my words go outside of me then return to my hole. The flowers in my hole fade as I shout, Flowers are blooming, flowers are blooming.

O

The verbs I use for cooking my hole are: "boil, roast, steam, simmer, decoct, burn." The objects used before the verbs are like the "inside"— the innermost heart, cabbage stuffing, blood sausage filling. You cook my "inside." You cook it well—my empty place which is like the inner part of an onion. I don't know how to stop my "inside" from burning up, so I always end up burning my invisible wick. Even when I boil my "inside," strangely, my heart becomes sick. You cook with "+heat" and "+water" based verbs, and the more you add "+heat" "+time" to the verbs, the more smoke rises from my hole and my heart gets cooked in the order of "boil, roast, steam, simmer, decoct, burn." In the end my whole body gets burnt. When you make my heart burn, my body also burns. The wall between my heart and body melts. The melted wall mushrooms again. Solid becomes gas. For your information, flower is a gas. It's a single-stemmed red gas. Heart is simultaneously a recipe and a cooked dish. When the smoke that burnt my heart pushes its way into your hole, you throw your chopsticks at it and say Go Away, You Stink! But then you don't particularly care for a sliced-up raw heart like a raw fish.

Today's dish—put several roots of hatred, add my mashed hole, and mix in shadow powder. Then boil the mixture down.

128

O

The holes of my body tremtremble when I follow the back of the truck fully
loaded with holes.
Holes! Whose body will you become?
The round darkness inside the holes!
Transparent tongues pant, for they want to become holes!

O

The hole is screaming. It's screaming on the phone. It's picking its nose.
The hole is deep in thought. It's sneering at something. It's ramming into
something. Behind the car many other cars line up. The hole doesn't get
shoved. It holds back its tears, unable to vomit. Vomit and gastric fluids
have reached the hole's neck. A police officer wearing leather gloves
comes running.

O

"I" is a name for a place of confinement in my body!
"I" is a name for all the things that don't appear outside the body's hole!
"I" is a name for the lady and gentleman who don't recognize the person
who lives in the body!
But is my hole sick? Is the mask of the hole sick?
If the hole dies, "I" die too. So "I" is a name for a single ripple etched onto
a lake. It's a name for a woman confined inside the hole's architecture.
Therefore, once again I'm a hole. I "do" hole. I'm someone who "does" a
hole voluntarily. All things are holes. All things "do" holes. All things have
just died, but the holes are alive. Holes will exist in the past and did exist
in the future. I'm the hole's playground, I'm the hole's misery, I'm the
hole's porter.

Plays w/ temporality

129

O

Red sap, bloody pus, mites are stuckstuck on the inner wall of a hole that leads up to the flower. The yellowish sebum, bloody pus on a newborn's skin. The small hole begins to rot. The hole gets bigger and bigger. Eventually the flower's head droops. The flower faded away after it tried to etch ripples in the air. Not a single cluster of the steam's ripples are visible—I wonder where they went after they floated in the air for a brief moment.

O

Dear Water! Fire! Wind! You who go up and down
the pitch-black starless alley, the chimney, the dark hole,
if you want to warm up the hole's darkness, you must get out of the body!
"There are so many repulsive people here. Let's go to a place where there is no one."
Why do people always say the same things?

Beneath my hole, the graves are wide open like laughing mouths.
Here, noxious gas and filthy water flow.
I go into my body and suffocate.
If I go through the entire hole, I will fall into a grave.
The hole is a stovepipe made with the vastness of the universe.
At the innermost part of the stovepipe, there is a stove, my heart.

O

Clean up the hole! God commands that not a single rat should be left in the hole.
A train loaded with rats arrives at my hole. Packs of rats run rampant.
I quickly put the hole in a coffin and nail it shut.

O

You who writes a letter of longing
is your name Gall Bladder? or Small Intestine?
If not, is it Esophagus?
Your name is a nameplate glued onto a hole.
I even have to love your hole.
You are a theater of hollowness.
Hole's church.
Hole factory.
I look at your face and can foresee the architecture of your hole.

Your tongue trembles delicately like rose moss
then the petals dangling at the end of the hole call my name as they fall.
So let's forget about the sewer today.
Your hole and my hole elegantly whinewhine.
Whining is the communication to and fro within the hole.

O

Hole, my beggar.
Hole, my prince.
Hole, my steel-enforced concrete that allows my body's movement.
Hole, my distant mandala.
The smooth traffic of the hole—that is existence.
Hole is my path, my truth, my beginning and end, so try your best to "do"
a hole for your hole.
My hole's identity, my hole's solitude, my hole's addiction.
Who's sitting in the control tower of my hole?
I go into my hole's maze, leaving a trail of thread. It's a longlong winding
path.

Yet, today, I want to send you down my path and have you implanted.
I want to live with you in my sewer.
A killer whale goes around the earth once then leaves again with its young.
At a deep place inside the hole, I slosh about like a well from which warm
water spouts up. I throb.

Hole labor—this is life.
Hole is the time bomb you have thrown.

You put your hand into my hole and stir.
Rose moss rollrolled up like a tongue at the end of the hole bloom.
The petals drool and dart their tongues towards my inside and outside.
The flower mixes the words, stirs the fragrances, and feeds the seeds to
keep them alive.
Again, for your information, the flower is a door. The door is a gas. It's
neither inside nor outside.
But then why do I have to spit out the seed to the outside only?
It's pointless pouring water into a jar whose bottom has fallen out. But the
flower only blooms in a jar without a bottom.

O

Keep the holes at a distance.
Abstain from the holes.
All holes are wolves.
The lessons of hole rabbis.

The night when my hole howls at the moon, I hold onto it and fall asleep
listening to its song.
When my hole sings the song in my knees, in my lymph nodes, in my
pelvis, in my groin, in my throat, in my nostrils, in my ears, the hole of the
continent over there replies.

A Tibetan pulls out one of my femurs and polishes a flute with it.

In a dream my song gets on a plane and flies through your hole, then lands.

I whimperwhimper and take off the hole as if taking off a heavy coat.

Music begins as I take off the hole. The imprisoned music unwinds the silk from its cocoon. The music traveling through the veins flows out at the end of the pen. Dear Hole, open the door. My hole doesn't open without my body's "doing." Dear Hole, "do" a hole. My hole opens as it opens yours. Music gushes out from the hole. The hole listens to the music. The music excavates all the graves hidden in the maze of my hole. The pipeline passing through the middle of the music begins to tremor. I need to tear your flesh to be able to listen to the music. With no hope, comfort, or meaning I soar up then fall deep down along with the tremors. Deep down there, the gigantic hole that has discarded its skin becomes even bigger. At that moment,

I drink butter by the Genghis Riverside and burn up like a corpse with a wick stuck down its throat. The dark lonely holes that my life has passed through begin to spew out candle drippings. Flame begins to flare up from the peak of the hole, which I refer to as this moment. Now at this moment fire gets kindled in the pit of the mound of my body, and the flames flare up along with the endless rapid currents of extinction. A flower blooms at one point in time. The mandala of flames wavers about at the plaza of darkness. When I go over the hole's climax the song of a song, the shout of a shout flow out by themselves. All the holes of my body, cry! Blood vessels burn till they turn white, my throat burns till it turns white.

A song flies up outside the hole.
The lids of manholes float in the air for a brief moment like graduation caps.

133

O

Dance is the sadness called upon by the music of my hole.
Dance is the cry that is called upon by the music rising up through my hole.
I dance like a pair of starved pink shoes that show up after midnight in the street.
I have come out of the hole, but my body is wearing a hole, the hole endlessly proliferates!
I must dance all the mazes.
I need to dance till the hole becomes sublime.
The hole dances like a snake with a feather attached to its head, rising up.
The tunnel, the tornado, the distant path have a song in them.
My hole dances. The flame dances. The ash that burnt me dances.
Hole, disappear into the dance!
The hole without hands or feet dances. It dances like incense. The sewer beneath my feet screams out sighs, and the wind pleads. Oh my god! All the leaves on the trees along the street are your ears.
When I lift up my lowly hole towards the sky, the golden spacecraft takes off from the hole.

I cry, laugh, shout at the plaza. My lips burst like a fountain. Sadness bursts.

holes, as existing outside

The hole is emitted nonstop to the outside. The mandala of rhythm floats up for a brief moment.
The sky lifts up my manhole's lid and starts a fire in my hole that is filled with indescribable rhythm.
Like a surfer I pass through the golden waves.

Then, soon, I plunge down like a hawk hit by an arrow, a snake that has lost its feather.

134

The world kneaded by music gets absorbed into the ground like spilled
water on the street.
The luminous dots of the music that used to go up and down at the edge
of the hole die like meteors.
The birds in my sleeves die. The sand mandala crumbles under the broom.
The coldcold charcoal, the night of the black shield rushes in.

O

There is a tunnel made by waves in Hawaii.
The tunnel was made by gigantic waves
that surge up then crash instantly in a circle.
When the blue sea lets out a sigh, the sea turns inside out
and the surfer on the yellow board goes through the sigh
The blue tunnel opens, yet crumbles!
One rolled up hole roams in the deep wave.

135

KIM, HYESOON is one of the most important contemporary poets of South Korea. She lives in Seoul and teaches creative writing at the Seoul Institute of the Arts. Kim was one of the first few women to be published in the literary journal, *Munhak kwa jisông* [Literature and Intellect]. During the 1970-80s, this journal and *Ch'angjak kwa pip'yông* [Creation and Criticism] were the two leaders of the intellectual and literary movement against the U.S.-backed military dictatorships. Kim first published not as a poet but as a critic. Her literary criticism won the *Tonga Daily*'s annual contest for new writers in 1978. She was a fourth-year college student at that time. When she went to collect her prize, someone approached her and said, "What makes you think you can be a critic with a maid's name like that?" Since then, Kim has steadily published poetry as well as criticism and received numerous prestigious literary awards. More translations of Kim's poetry can be found in *When the Plug Gets Unplugged* (Tinfish 2005), *Anxiety of Words* (Zephyr, 2006), and *Mommy Must Be a Fountain of Feathers* (Action Books, 2008). Some of her poems are also available in Spanish and German. Kim has recently read at Taipei Poetry Festival, Poetry International Festival Rotterdam, and Poesiefestival Berlin.

CHOI, DON MEE is the author of *The Morning News is Exciting* (Action Books, 2010). She lives and works in Seattle.

ACKNOWLEDGEMENTS

All the Garbage of the World, Unite! has been translated from the following titles by Kim Hyesoon:

Tangshin ûi ch'ôt [Your First]. Seoul: Munhak kwa chisông sa, 2008
"*Maenhol inryu*" [Manhole Humanity] in *Chaûm kwa moûm*. Seoul, 2009

Translator's Acknowledgements:
The translation of this project was supported by a generous grant from the Daesan Foundation, Seoul.

Thank you to the editors of the following journals in which some of the translations first appeared: *Azalea: Journal of Korean Literature and Culture, Jubilat, Peaches & Bats, Poetry International Web,* and *Tinfish.*

My sincere gratitude to Joyelle McSweeney and Johannes Göransson for their continuous support of Kim Hyesoon's poetry/translation. Special thanks to Kimberly Koga for her careful reading and feedback. I am deeply indebted to Deborah Woodard and Kim Hyesoon for their many wonderful editorial suggestions that helped to make these translations what they are now. And, last but not least, I thank Steve Bradbury for his unconditional support and enthusiasm.